WORKBOOK STARTER

Herbert Puchta, Jeff Stranks & Peter Lewis-Jones

CAMBRIDGE
UNIVERSITY PRESS

Acknowledgements

The authors and publishers acknowledge the following sources of copyright material and are grateful for the permissions granted. While every effort has been made, it has not always been possible to identify the sources of all the material used, or to trace all copyright holders. If any omissions are brought to our notice, we will be happy to include the appropriate acknowledgements on reprinting.

Corpus

Development of this publication has made use of the Cambridge English Corpus (CEC). The CEC is a computer database of contemporary spoken and written English, which currently stands at over one billion words. It includes British English, American English and other varieties of English. It also includes the Cambridge Learner Corpus, developed in collaboration with Cambridge English Language Assessment. Cambridge University Press has built up the CEC to provide evidence about language use that helps to produce better language teaching materials.

English Profile

This product is informed by the English Vocabulary Profile, built as part of English Profile, a collaborative programme designed to enhance the learning, teaching and assessment of English worldwide. Its main funding partners are Cambridge University Press and Cambridge English Language Assessment and its aim is to create a 'profile' for English linked to the Common European Framework of Reference for Languages (CEF). English Profile outcomes, such as the English Vocabulary Profile, will provide detailed information about the language that learners can be expected to demonstrate at each CEF level, offering a clear benchmark for learners' proficiency. For more information, please visit www.englishprofile.org

Cambridge Dictionaries

Cambridge dictionaries are the world's most widely used dictionaries for learners of English. The dictionaries are available in print and online at dictionary.cambridge.org. Copyright © Cambridge University Press, reproduced with permission.

The publishers are grateful to the following for permission to reproduce copyright photographs and material:

T = Top, B = Below, L = Left, R = Right, C = Centre, B/G = Background

p. 5 (TL): Peshkova / Getty Images; p. 5 (TL): © Michael Dwyer / Alamy; p. 5 (TL): © Rrrainbow / Alamy; p. 5 (TL): © Zoonar GmbH / Alamy; p. 5 (TL): Foodcollection / Getty Images; p. 5 (TL): © RTimages / Alamy; p. 5 (TL): © The Picture Pantry / Alamy; p. 5 (TL): fStop Images / Getty Images; p. 5 (TL): © Tetra Images / Alamy; p. 5 (TL): © YAY Media AS / Alamy; p. 5 (TL): vsl / Shutterstock; p. 5 (BL): © Ivan Vdovin / Alamy; p. 5 (BL): © Tom Grundy / Alamy; p. 5 (BL): © Tetra Images / Alamy; p. 5 (BL): © russ witherington / Alamy; p. 5 (BL): © Nadiya Teslyuk / Alamy; p. 6 (TR): Jose Luis Pelaez Inc / Getty Images; p. 6 (BR): © TongRo Images / Alamy; p. 7 (TL): koya79 / Getty Images; p. 7 (TL): © Archideaphoto / Alamy; p. 7 (TL): © RTimages / Alamy; p. 7 (TL): Datacraft Co Ltd / Getty Images; p. 7 (TL): © Dmitry Rukhlenko / Alamy; p. 7 (TL): Hemera Technologies / Getty Images; p. 7 (TL): © Anton Starikov / Alamy; p. 7 (TL): © aviv avivbenor / Alamy; p. 7 (BL): © Héctor Sánchez / Alamy; p. 7 (BL): © Zoonar GmbH / Alamy; p. 7 (BR): © Robert Fried / Alamy; p. 7 (BR): Siri Stafford / Getty Images; p. 10 (BL): © Radius Images / Alamy; p. 11 (BL): filipefrazao / Getty Images; p. 11 (BL): © PHOVOIR / Alamy; p. 11 (BL): © wareham.nl (sport) / Alamy; p. 11 (BL): © E.D. Torial / Alamy; p. 11 (BL): © Zoonar GmbH / Alamy; p. 11 (BL): STOCK4B/ Getty Images; p. 13 (TR): © wiba / Alamy; p. 13 (TR): © HolgerBurmeister / Alamy; p. 14 (CR): © James Davies / Alamy; p. 14 (CR): AFP / Getty Images; p. 15 (TR): Kali Nine LLC / Getty Images; p. 15 (TR): Kali Nine LLC / Getty Images; p. 15 (TR): omgimages / Getty Images; p. 16 (TL): Laurence Cartwright Photograph/ Getty Images; p. 16 (TL): © Bloomimage/Corbis; p. 16 (TL): Juanmonino/ Getty Images; p. 16 (TL): © Tetra Images / Alamy; p. 16 (TL): PeopleImages.com / Getty Images; p. 17 (TL): Kai_Wong / Getty Images; p. 17 (TL): Lya_Cattel/ Getty Images; p. 17 (TL): Thierry Levenq / Getty Images; p. 17 (TL): © Horizon Images/Motion / Alamy; p. 19 (TL): © Imagestate Media Partners Limited - Impact Photos / Alamy; p. 22 (CR): © ZUMA Press, Inc. / Alamy; p. 24 (TL): © age fotostock / Alamy; p. 27 (CL): Ron Levine / Getty Images; p. 27 (TL): © Katrina Brown / Alamy; p. 27 (TR): Hill Street Studios / Getty Images; p. 31 (CR): © Archideaphoto / Alamy; p. 31 (CR): © Y H Lim / Alamy; p. 31 (CR): Charlie Dean / Getty Images; p. 31 (CR): Christopher Steer / Getty Images; p. 31 (CR): PhotoAlto / Laurence Mouton / Getty Images; p. 31 (CR): Maciej Toporowicz, NYC/ Getty Images; p. 32 (TR): © Eric Audras/Onoky/ Corbis; p. 37 (TR): Paul Bradbury / Getty Images; p. 40 (TR): © Image Source / Alamy; p. 41 (TR): © OJO Images Ltd / Alamy; p. 44 (BR): © Danny Smythe / Alamy; p. 44 (BR): flyfloor / Getty Images; p. 44 (BR): satori13/ Getty Images; p. 44 (BR): © Art Directors & TRIP / Alamy; p. 44 (BR): © Y H Lim / Alamy; p. 51 (TR): © Victorio Castellani / Alamy; p. 51 (TR): John Rowley/ Getty Images; p. 54 (TR): Andresr / Shutterstock; p. 54 (TR): © debbiewibowo / RooM the Agency / Corbis; p. 54 (TR): © Beau Lark/Corbis; p. 54 (TR):© Image Source / Corbis; p. 55 (TR): Tetra Images / Getty Images; p. 59 (TR): Luna Vandoorne / Shutterstock; p. 61 (BL): © Radius Images / Alamy; p. 63 (BR): Tetra Images / Getty Images; p. 66 (TL): © RTimages / Alamy; p. 67 (CL): © Michael Burrell / Alamy; p. 68 (CR): © Action Plus Sports Images / Alamy; p. 68 (CR): © Bob Daemmrich / Alamy; p. 69 (TR): Gerville Hall / Getty Images; p. 69 (TR): Ken Reid / Getty Images; p. 70 (BL): © RTimages / Alamy; p. 76 (TR): Hero Images / Getty Images; p. 77 (BL): Westend61 / Getty Images; p. 85 (CL): © Finnbarr Webster / Alamy; p. 85 (CL): © Edd Westmacott / Alamy; p. 85 (CL): © Elena Butinova / Alamy; p. 85 (CL): © HERA FOOD / Alamy; p. 85 (CL): © Keith Leighton / Alamy; p. 85 (CL): © Indigo Photo Agency / Alamy; p. 85 (CL): © Keith Leighton / Alamy; p. 85 (CL): © LAMB / Alamy; p. 85 (CL): © D. Hurst / Alamy; p. 85 (CL): © Nikreates / Alamy; p. 85 (CL): © Miles Davies / Alamy; p. 86 (TR): Pamela Moore / Getty Images; p. 86 (TR): Tetra Images / Getty Images; p. 86 (TR): valmas / Getty Images; p. 86 (TR): Karly Pope / Getty Images; p. 86 (TR): raphotography/ Getty Images; p. 86 (CR): © imageBROKER / Alamy; p. 88 (BL): Jacobs Stock Photography / Getty Images; p. 90 (BL): © Mike Blenkinsop / Alamy; p. 91 (TR): © GL Archive / Alamy; p. 95 (TL): © AF archive / Alamy; p. 95 (TR): © AF archive / Alamy; p. 96 (TL): © Pictorial Press Ltd / Alamy; p. 97 (CL): © Pierre Auguste Renoir / Getty Images; p. 97 (CR): © Chris Hellier / Alamy; p. 99 (BR): Andersen Ross / Getty Images; p. 101 (TR): Izabela Habur / Getty Images; p. 104 (CR):   The Indianapolis Fire Department; p. 104 (CR): BPM Media; p. 105 (BL):   © Stocktrek Images, Inc / Alamy; p. 105 (BL):© Arterra Picture Library / Alamy; p. 105 (BL): © Stocktrek Images, Inc. / Alamy; p. 106 (CR): © PhotoAlto sas / Alamy; p. 107 (Top): Science Photo Library - MARK GARLICK/ Getty Images; p. 107 (Top): Denis Kozlenko / Getty Images; p. 107 (Top): Raul_Wong / Getty Images; p. 112 (CR): © Cultura Creative (RF) / Alamy; p. 112 (CR): Grant Faint / Getty Images; p. 114 (TL): kyoshino / Getty Images; p. 117 (DR): Stephen Saks / Getty Images.

Cover photographs by: (L): ©Tim Gainey/Alamy Stock Photo; (R): ©Yuliya Koldovska/Shutterstock.

The publishers are grateful to the following illustrators:
Christos Skaltsas (hyphen) 6, 8 (L), 10, 26, 28, 35 (L), 38, 39 (R), 43, 46, 50, 52, 56, 57, 59, 60, 64, 65, 67, 70, 71, 75, 84, 94, 103, 109, 111 and Zaharias Papadopoulos (hyphen) 8 (R), 12, 16, 20, 35 (TR), 39 (L), 44, 48, 58, 92, 112

The publishers are grateful to the following contributors:
hyphen: editorial, design and project management; Leon Chambers: audio recordings; Karen Elliott: Pronunciation sections; Matt Norton: Get it right! exercises

CONTENTS

WELCOME

The alphabet

1 🔊02 **Listen and write the names and the cities.**

Names

0 *Harry*

1 _ _ _ _

2 _ _ _ _ _

3 _ _ _ _

4 _ _ _ _ _

5 _ _ _ _

Cities

1 _ _ _ _ _

2 _ _ _ _

3 _ _ _ _ _

4 _ _ _ _ _

5 _ _ _ _

6 _ _ _ _ _ _ _

2 **Match to make the words.**

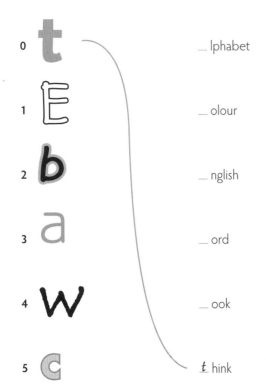

0 **t**   _ lphabet

1 **E**   _ olour

2 **b**   _ nglish

3 **a**   _ ord

4 **W**   _ ook

5 **c**   *t* hink

Colours

1 🔊03 **Listen and write the colours. Then colour.**

0 *b l a c k*   6 _ _ _ _ _ _

1 _ _ _ _ _   7 _ _ _ _ _

2 _ _ _ _ _   8 _ _ _ _ _

3 _ _ _ _ _   9 _ _ _ _ _

4 _ _ _ _ _   10 _ _ _ _ _

5 _ _ _ _ _

2 **Find and ⟨circle⟩ eleven colours in the word snake.**

greenorangeblackgreyblueredpurplepinkbrownwhiteyellow

International words

1 Unscramble the letters to make words.

0 trapior *airport*

1 sub _____

2 facé _____

3 -fiiw _____

4 ishus _____

5 bolaotfl _____

6 rbumagerh _____

7 thole _____

8 iytc _____

9 openh _____

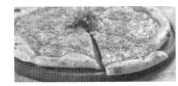

10 zizap _____

11 tranaurest _____

12 cinadswh _____

13 axit _____

14 inevilesto _____

15 bleatt _____

2 ◀))04 Listen and put the words in order.

a ☐ hamburger
b ☐ airport
c ☐ phone
d ☐ pizza
e ☐ café
f ☐ television
g ☐ tablet
h [1] sushi
i ☐ hotel
j ☐ city

SUMMING UP

1 ◀))05 Listen and draw.

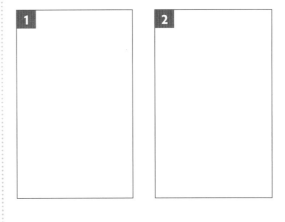

1	2

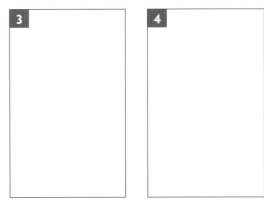

3	4

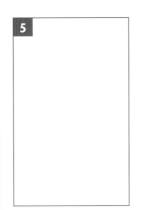

5	6

Articles: *a* and *an*

1 (Circle) the correct options.

0 *a* /(*an*) orange bus
1 *a* / *an* Italian city
2 *a* / *an* American TV
3 *a* / *an* white tablet
4 *a* / *an* English actor
5 *a* / *an* hamburger
6 *a* / *an* black taxi
7 *a* / *an* phone
8 *a* / *an* grey airport
9 *a* / *an* red bus

2 Write the words in the list in the correct columns. How many more words can you write?

actor | airport | apple | ~~city~~ | hamburger
hotel | orange | TV

a	an
city	

The day

1 Look at the pictures and complete the phrases.

0 Good *morning*

1 Good _ _ _ _ _ _

2 Good _ _ _ _ _ _ _ _

3 Good _ _ _ _ _ _ _ _ _ _

Saying *Hello* and *Goodbye*

1 Write the words in the list under the pictures.

Bye | Good afternoon | Good evening | Good morning | Good night | ~~Hello~~ | Hi | See you

_____ *Hello* _____   _____

_____   _____

_____   _____

_____   _____

Classroom objects

1 Match the pictures with the words in the list. Write 1–10 in the boxes.

1 ~~book~~ | 2 chair | 3 computer | 4 desk
5 door | 6 pen | 7 pencil | 8 projector
9 board | 10 window

A ☐   B ☐

C ☐   D ☐

E ☐   F ☐

G ☐   H ☐

I ☐   J 1

2 Find the words from Exercise 1 in the word search.

W	B	I	T	T	B	O	A	R	D
I	B	O	V	N	O	W	T	O	P
N	O	I	R	Q	O	M	K	T	E
D	P	Y	T	D	K	B	L	C	N
O	L	S	T	B	Z	K	S	E	D
W	N	V	M	I	Q	G	J	J	U
E	S	R	E	T	U	P	M	O	C
X	J	O	V	C	H	A	I	R	Z
L	R	O	L	I	C	N	E	P	M
G	S	D	H	X	E	K	L	Q	B

SUMMING UP

1 🔊06 Put the dialogues in order. Then listen and check.

Dialogue 1

1	CONNOR	Good morning, Mr Davis.
☐	CONNOR	I'm fine. And you?
☐	MR DAVIS	Hello, Connor. How are you?
☐	MR DAVIS	I'm great, thanks.

Dialogue 2

☐	LEWIS	Yeah, have a good day.
☐	LEWIS	Bye, Paula.
☐	PAULA	Bye, Lewis. See you later.

Dialogue 3

☐	LUCY	I'm fine, thank you.
☐	LUCY	Bye, Mrs Edwards.
1	LUCY	Good afternoon, Mrs Edwards.
☐	MRS EDWARDS	Good. I'll see you in class.
☐	MRS EDWARDS	Hello, Lucy. How are you?

2 Write short dialogues.

OLIVIA   *Hello.* _____

JIM   _____

BRIAN   _____

OLIVIA   _____

TIM   _____

DAD   _____

Numbers 0–20

1 Write the numbers in the boxes.

1	four	4		12	seven	
2	eight			13	sixteen	
3	twenty			14	eighteen	
4	five			15	ten	
5	twelve			16	fourteen	
6	six			17	three	
7	eleven			18	thirteen	
8	one			19	seventeen	
9	fifteen			20	two	
10	nineteen			21	nine	
11	zero					

Plural nouns

1 How many? Find, count and write the plurals.

book | chair | child | computer | door | ~~man~~
pencil | pen | phone | window | woman

0	eight	*men*
1	three	
2	seven	
3	fifteen	
4	eighteen	
5	two	
6	one	
7	zero	
8	twelve	
9	four	
10	six	

Classroom language

1 Circle the correct options.

0 *Close your books. /*
What does this mean?

1 *Put up your hand. /*
Close your books.

2 *Listen. /*
That's right.

3 *Work with a partner. /*
That's wrong.

4 *Listen. /*
Look at the picture.

5 *Work with a partner. /*
Put up your hand.

6 *Open your books. /*
Look at the picture.

Numbers 20–100

1 Write the numbers.

0	seventy	70
1	thirty	
2	forty	
3	ninety	
4	a hundred	
5	fifty	
6	twenty	
7	sixty	
8	eighty	
9	thirty-four	
10	sixty-eight	
11	twenty-one	
12	ninety-nine	
13	fifty-three	

2 ◀))07 **Listen and write the numbers.**

a _thirty-four_
b _____
c _____
d _____
e _____
f _____
g _____
h _____
i _____
j _____
k _____

Messages

1 ◀))08 **Listen to the messages and (circle) the correct options.**

Message 1

Hi, Luke

Message from Paul [1]Jones / James.
His house number is [2]7 / 8.
The bus number is [3]8 / 9.
His phone number is [4]0987868758 / 0987886758.

Message 2

Hi, Debbie

Message from [5]Claire / Clare [6]Green / Greene.
Her house number is [7]44 / 34.
The bus number is [8]15 / 16.
Her phone number is
01244 [9]7564453 / 5634453.

SUMMING UP

1 ◀))09 **Listen and complete the messages.**

Message 1

Hi, Martin

Message from Mr [0] _Cleverly_.
His house number is [1]_____
The bus number is [2]_____
His phone number is [3]_____

Message 2

Hi, Chloe

Message from Jane [4]_____.
Her house number is [5]_____.
The bus number is [6]_____.
Her phone number is [7]_____.

1 | ONE WORLD

GRAMMAR
Question words   `SB page 14`

1 ★☆☆ **Complete the sentences with the correct question words.**

> 0   *What* is your name?

> 1 _____ old are you?

> 2 _____ are you from?

> 3 _____ is your favourite athlete?

> 4 _____ is he/she your favourite athlete?

2 ★★★ **Write answers to the questions in Exercise 1 so they are true for you.**

0   *My name is* _____
1   _____
2   _____
3   _____
4   _____

Pronunciation
/h/ or /w/ in question words
Go to page 118.

3 ★★☆ **Look at the pictures and circle the correct words.**

0   *He / She / It* is happy.

1   *We / You / I* are friends.

2   *They / We / You* are Japanese.

3   *She / He / It* is eleven.

4   *I / She / We* am Carla.

5   *We / They / You* are Fred.

6   *We / You / They* are sisters.

7   *I / It / You* is the Brazilian flag.

to be `SB page 15`

4 ★ Complete the table with the words in the list.

~~am~~ | are | are | are | is | is | is

0	I	*am*	Paul.
1	You		13.
2	He		happy.
3	She		from Mexico.
4	It		Japanese.
5	We		sisters.
6	They		friends.

5 ★★ Complete the sentences with the verb *to be*. Use short forms.

0 You ___'re___ Russian.

1 I _____ Portuguese.

2 We _____ Mexican.

3 They _____ Brazilian.

4 He _____ Spanish.

5 She _____ American.

6 ★★ Rewrite the sentences using short forms.

0 It is a Turkish flag.
It's a Turkish flag.

1 She is Russian.

2 You are a good friend.

3 They are British.

4 We are from London.

5 I am Paul. What is your name?

6 He is 12 today.

GET IT RIGHT! 👁
Subject–verb agreement with *be*

We use the form of *be* that agrees with the subject.
✓ *They **are** from Italy.*
✗ *They **is** from Italy.*

Correct the sentences.

0 There are a beautiful beach.
There is a beautiful beach.

1 The lessons is for two hours.

2 It are cold today.

3 Are the English player good?

4 We's from France.

5 My favourite country are the USA.

VOCABULARY

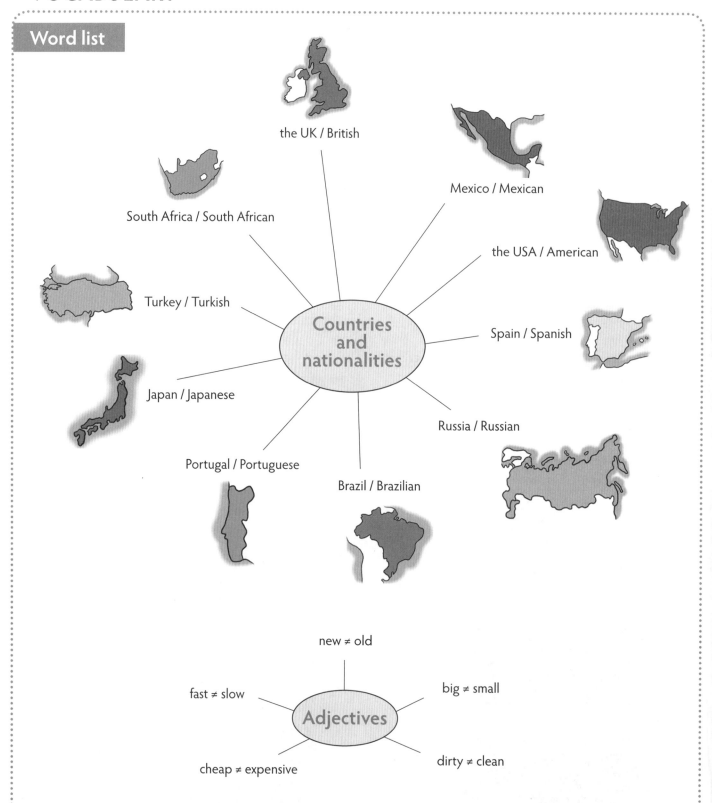

the UK / British

Mexico / Mexican

the USA / American

South Africa / South African

Spain / Spanish

Turkey / Turkish

Countries and nationalities

Japan / Japanese

Russia / Russian

Portugal / Portuguese

Brazil / Brazilian

new ≠ old

fast ≠ slow

big ≠ small

Adjectives

cheap ≠ expensive

dirty ≠ clean

Key words in context

athlete	Usain Bolt is a famous **athlete** from Jamaica.
country	Mexico is a beautiful **country**.
fan	I'm a great **fan** of Jennifer Lawrence.
flag	The American **flag** is red, white and blue.
nationality	What's your **nationality**?
player	Gareth Bale is my favourite football **player**.

Countries and nationalities
SB page 14

1 ★ **Find ten countries in the word search. Then write the countries.**

N	H	I	S	O	C	I	X	E	M
I	B	R	A	Z	I	L	S	G	E
A	B	V	J	A	S	K	O	J	T
K	C	N	A	M	P	S	U	I	U
U	Y	E	I	F	A	L	T	C	R
E	M	Z	S	E	S	L	H	G	K
H	P	B	S	K	P	R	A	H	E
T	H	E	U	S	A	U	F	X	Y
A	C	V	R	W	I	Z	R	B	J
E	J	A	P	A	N	A	I	T	Q
R	R	K	A	Y	H	B	C	N	M
G	P	O	R	T	U	G	A	L	D

0 *Brazil*

1 _____

2 _____

3 _____

4 _____

5 _____

6 _____

7 _____

8 _____

9 _____

2 ★★ **Complete the words.**

0 Oliver's from Cape Town. He's
   South Afric *an* .

1 He's from London. He's Briti_____ .

2 I'm from Mexico City. I'm
   Mexic_____ .

3 She's from New York. She's
   Americ_____ .

4 They're from Barcelona. They're
   Span_____ .

5 You're from Moscow. You're
   Russi_____ .

6 My mum is from Rio. She's
   Brazili_____ .

7 Our teacher is from Lisbon. He's
   Portugu_____ .

8 Haruki is from Tokyo. He's Japan_____ .

9 They're from Istanbul.
   They're Turk_____ .

Adjectives SB page 17

3 ★ **Write the adjectives under the pictures.**

big | cheap | clean | dirty | ~~expensive~~
fast | new | old | slow | small

£1,000,000

The car is …

0 *expensive* .

1 _____ .

2 _____ .

3 _____ .

4 _____ .

£50

The car is …

5 _____ .

6 _____ .

7 _____ .

8 _____ .

9 _____ .

4 ★★ **Put the words in order to make sentences.**

0 book / English / My / new / is
   My English book is new.

1 red / Her / is / pen

   _____

2 is / house / old / Our

   _____

3 fast / bikes / Their / are

   _____

4 big / school / Our / is

   _____

5 My / small / bedroom / is

   _____

6 car / Her / expensive / is

   _____

READING

1 REMEMBER AND CHECK Complete the table. Then look at the website on page 13 of the Student's Book and check your answers.

Name	Age	Country	City	Favourite athlete
Pedro	10			
Brittany				
Oleg				
Haruka				

2 Read the text quickly. Where are they from? Match the names with the countries.

0	Juan	c	a	Turkey
1	Mary Lou		b	South Africa
2	Ibrahim		c	Mexico
3	Rebecca		d	the USA
4	Lucy		e	the UK

Hi, my name's Juan. I'm from Acapulco. I'm Mexican. I'm twelve years old.
My favourite athlete is James Rodriguez. He's a football player from Colombia. He's great.

My name's Mary Lou. I'm ten years old. I'm American. I'm from Dallas.
My favourite athlete is Rafael Nadal. He's a tennis player. He's Spanish. He's awesome.

Hi, I'm Ibrahim. I'm from Istanbul. I'm Turkish. I'm eleven years old.
My favourite athlete is Ellie Simmonds. She's a swimmer from the UK. She's really fast.

My name's Rebecca. I'm twelve years old. I'm South African. I'm from Cape Town.
My favourite athlete is Marta. She's a footballer. She's Brazilian. She's amazing.

My name's Lucy. I'm eleven years old. I'm British. I'm from Liverpool.
My favourite athlete is Usain Bolt. He's a runner. He's Jamaican. He's great.

3 Read the text again. Mark the sentences T (true) or F (false).

0	Juan is from Mexico City.	F
1	Juan's favourite athlete is a football player.	
2	Mary Lou is ten.	
3	Mary Lou's favourite athlete is a Brazilian tennis player.	
4	Ibrahim is from Turkey.	
5	Ellie Simmonds is an American swimmer.	
6	Rebecca is eleven.	
7	Rebecca is from Brazil.	
8	Lucy is from Liverpool.	
9	Lucy's favourite athlete is a woman.	

DEVELOPING WRITING

About me

1 Read the mini questionnaire. Then complete the text with the missing words.

Bournemouth Sports Academy

Be the Best – Summer Sports Camp on the English Coast!
Tennis, football, volleyball, athletics – we can help you be the best!

We want to know all about you.

What's your name?   *Pedro Velho*

Where are you from?   *Nova Friburgo in Brazil*

How old are you?   *12*

Who's your favourite athlete?   *Lionel Messi*

Who's your favourite pop star?   *will.i.am*

Hi, my name is ⁰_____ *Pedro* _____.
I'm Brazilian. I'm from ¹_____ .
I'm ²_____ years old.
My favourite athlete is
³_____ .
He's a football player from Argentina.
He's amazing. I love football!
I love music, too. My favourite pop star is
⁴_____ . He's awesome.

2 Use the text to complete the questionnaire.

Hi, my name is Amy Davies. I'm American.
I'm from Seattle. I'm eleven years old.
My favourite athlete is Serena Williams.
She's a tennis player from the USA.
She's awesome. I love tennis!
I love music, too. My favourite pop star
is Taylor Swift. She's great.

Bournemouth Sports Academy

Be the Best – Summer Sports Camp on the English Coast
Tennis, football, volleyball, athletics – we can help you be the best!

We want to know all about you.

What's your name?   ⁰ *Amy Davies*

Where are you from?   ¹_____

How old are you?   ²_____

Who's your favourite athlete?   ³_____

Who's your favourite pop star?   ⁴_____

3 Complete the text about you.

Hi, my name is ¹_____ . I'm ²_____ . I'm from ³_____ .
I'm ⁴_____ years old. My favourite athlete is ⁵_____ . He's / She's a
⁶_____ from ⁷_____ . He's / She's ⁸_____ . I love ⁹_____ !
I love music, too. My favourite pop star is ¹⁰_____ . He's / She's ¹¹_____ .

LISTENING

1 🔊 12 **Listen to the dialogue. Number the people in the order you hear them.**

1

2 🔊 12 **Listen again and write the names in the list under the pictures in Exercise 1.**

Ayse | Keiko | Kayla | Roberto | Steve

3 (Circle) **the correct answers (A or B).**

0   Keiko is from …
   (A) Japan.   B   Lisbon.
1   Roberto is from …
   A   Beijing.   B   Lisbon.
2   Ayse is from …
   A   Istanbul.   B   Moscow.
3   Steve is from …
   A   London.   B   Cape Town.
4   Kayla is from …
   A   London.   B   Cape Town.

DIALOGUE

1   **Choose the correct answers (A, B or C) to complete the dialogue.**

BOY   Hi, what's your name?
GIRL   I'm 0   A   12.
                  B   Brazil.
                  (C) Julia.
BOY   And where are you from?
GIRL   1   A   I'm American.
              B   I'm 10.
              C   Sara.
BOY   What city are you from?
GIRL   2   A   Japan.
              B   New York.
              C   Mexico.
BOY   New York's a beautiful city.
GIRL   3   A   Yes, I am.
              B   Yes, it is.
              C   Yes, they are.
BOY   Who's your favourite singer?
GIRL   4   A   Pharrell Williams.
              B   Ronaldo.
              C   Yes.
BOY   Why is he your favourite singer?
GIRL   5   A   No.
              B   Yes.
              C   Because he's awesome.
BOY   Nice to meet you, Julia.
GIRL   6   A   Yes.
              B   No.
              C   Nice to meet you, too.

PHRASES FOR FLUENCY   SB page 19

1   **Match the phrases 1–4 with their similar meanings a–d.**

1   How's it going?   a   Goodbye.
2   See you later.   b   How are you?
3   I know.   c   Great.
4   That is so awesome!   d   You're right.

2   **Use the phrases 1–4 in Exercise 1 to complete the dialogues.**

1   A   Hi, Connor. _____
    B   I'm fine, thanks.

2   A   Bye, Janice.
    B   Bye, Tim. _____

3   A   This is my new laptop.
    B   _____

4   A   Liam's a great football player.
    B   _____

Sum it up

The Big World Quiz

1 Where do you find these things?

1

A the USA
B the UK
C Spain

2

A the USA
B Turkey
C Russia

3

A Mexico
B Brazil
C Japan

4

A Japan
B Portugal
C Spain

2 Where do they say 'hello' like this?

1 'How's it going?'
A the USA
B Portugal
C Brazil
2 'Buenos Dias'
A Spain
B Turkey
C the UK
3 'Konnichiwa'
A Russia
B South Africa
C Japan
4 'Merhaba'
A Russia
B Turkey
C Mexico

3 Where are these capital cities?

1 Lisbon
A Portugal
B Brazil
C Mexico
2 Pretoria
A the UK
B Japan
C South Africa
3 Ankara
A the USA
B Turkey
C Spain
4 Brasilia
A Mexico
B Russia
C Brazil

4 Who is from …

1 Brazil?
A Marta
B Tony Kroos
C James Rodriguez
2 the UK?
A Serena Williams
B Usain Bolt
C Ellie Simonds
3 Russia?
A Bruno Mars
B Maria Sharapova
C will.i.am
4 the USA?
A Taylor Swift
B Gareth Bale
C Lionel Messi

2 | I FEEL HAPPY

GRAMMAR

to be (negative, singular and plural)
SB page 22

1 ★☆☆ (Circle) the correct form of *to be*.

0 Joe (is) / *am* happy today. It *'s* / *'re* his birthday.

1 We *am* / *are* excited. We *'s* / *'re* on holiday.

2 It *'s* / *'m* late. I *'s* / *'m* tired.

3 Helen and Amanda *is* / *are* happy today. They *is* / *are* in the tennis team.

4 You *are* / *is* angry.

5 It *is* / *are* hot here.

2 ★★☆ Complete the sentences with the correct negative form of *to be*.

0 I ___'m not___ tired. I'm worried.

1 James _____ happy. He's bored.

2 Sarah and Jane _____ worried. They're excited.

3 We _____ angry with you. We're worried about you. That's all.

4 Susan _____ happy at her new school. Her new classmates _____ very friendly.

5 It _____ hot in here. It's cold. Close the window.

6 I _____ hungry. I'm thirsty.

to be (questions and short answers)
SB page 23

3 ★★☆ (Circle) the correct form of *to be*.

1 A *Is I* (Are) Martin and Matt with you?
  B No, they *isn't* / *aren't*.

2 A *Am* / *Is* I in your team?
  B Yes, you *is* / *are*.

3 A *Am* / *Are* you on the beach now?
  B No, we *isn't* / *aren't*.

4 A *Is* / *Are* Nick at home?
  B No, he *isn't* / *aren't*.

5 A *Is* / *Are* Emma at school today?
  B Yes, she *is* / *are*.

6 A *Am* / *Are* you American?
  B No, I *'m not* / *aren't*.

4 ★★☆ Write the questions. Then write answers to the questions so they are true for you.

0 your name / Mary?
  Is your name Mary?   *No, it isn't.*

1 you / 15?
  _____   _____

2 you / Mexican?
  _____   _____

3 your mum / a teacher?
  _____   _____

4 your dad / from England?
  _____   _____

5 you / happy?
  _____   _____

6 your / classmates / friendly?
  _____   _____

5 ★★☆ Complete the text messages with the correct form of *to be*.

Hi, Kathy. 0 ___Are___ you happy?
1 _____ your new school OK?
2 _____ the students friendly?
3 _____ it sunny there? It
4 _____ (✗) sunny here ☹.
School 5 _____ (✗) the same
without you ☹. Text me.

Hi, Marie. I 6 _____ (✓) happy ☺.
School 7 _____ (✓) very different
here in Australia. There 8 _____ (✓)
ten boys and twelve girls in my class.
The girls 9 _____ (✓) very friendly
but the boys 10 _____ (✗) ☹.
It 11 _____ (✓) very hot and sunny
here ☺. And guess what? There
12 _____ (✓) a swimming pool in
the playground ☺. It 13 _____ (✗)
all bad!

Object pronouns SB page 25

6 ★ ☆ ☆ **Complete the sentences with** *me*, *him*, *her*, *us*, *you* **and** *them*.

My new school

0 My new school is excellent. I really like
    ___*it*___ .

1 The school dinners are great. I like _____ .

2 Our English teacher is Mrs Smith. I like
    _____ .

3 We are good students. Mrs Smith is very happy
    with _____ .

4 Tim is my best friend here. He's great. I really like
    _____ .

5 I'm friendly. My classmates like _____ .

6 Are you friendly? Do your classmates like
    _____ ?

7 ★★ ☆ **Complete the dialogues so they are true for you. Use the correct object pronouns.**

0 **A** Do you like ___*Neymar*___ ? (name of a sports person)

  B Yes, I really like ___*him*___ .

1 **A** Do you like _____ ? (name of a girl singer)

  B Yes, I like _____ . She's great.

2 **A** Do you like _____ ? (name of pop group)

  B No, I don't like _____ . They're terrible.

3 **A** Do you like _____ ? (name of an actor)

  B Yes, I like _____ . He's an excellent actor.

4 **A** Do you like _____ ? (name of a film)

  B Yes, I like _____ . It's very funny.

8 ★★★ **Write questions with** *like* **and the word in brackets. Then write answers to the questions so they are true for you.**

0 Katy Perry? (you)

  Do you like Katy Perry?

  Yes, I like her. She's a great singer.

1 the TV programme *Dr Who*? (you)

  _____

  _____

2 football? (your dad)

  _____

  _____

3 One Direction? (your best friend)

  _____

  _____

4 Taylor Swift? (you)

  _____

  _____

5 comedy films? (your mum)

  _____

  _____

6 the song 'Good Feeling' by Flo Rida? (you)

  _____

  _____

7 talent shows? (your mum and dad)

  _____

  _____

GET IT RIGHT!
Object pronouns

We use *it* **in the singular and** *them* **in the plural**

✓ *I don't want this sweet. You have* ***it***.

✓ *I don't want these sweets. You have* ***them***.

✗ *I don't want these sweets. You have it.*

Circle the correct options.

0 This is my school. I like *it* / *them*.

1 I play computer games. I like *it* / *them*.

2 My dad has a really cool phone. I want *it* / *them*!

3 My country is small but I like *it* / *them* a lot.

4 One Direction? I don't like *it* / *them*.

5 My friends are here. I play football with *it* / *them* every afternoon.

6 Here is my homework. I finished *it* / *them* this morning.

VOCABULARY

Adjectives to describe feelings

cold

sad

bored

hot

worried

angry

hungry

excited

tired

thirsty

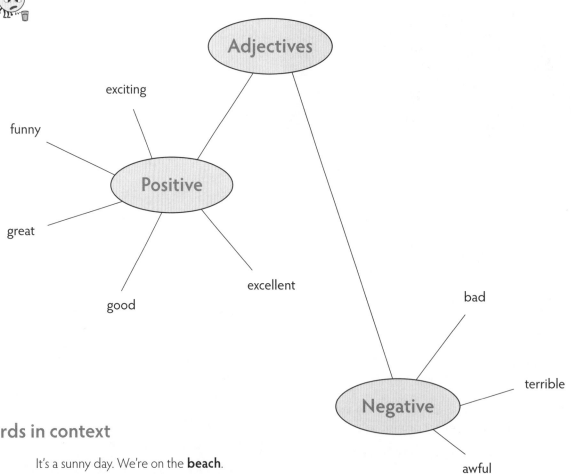

Adjectives

Positive

exciting
funny
great
good
excellent

Negative

bad
terrible
awful

Key words in context

beach	It's a sunny day. We're on the **beach**.
bus	I'm on the **bus** with my friends.
club	It's a **club**. They do lots of different activities there.
film	I like comedy **film**s. They're funny.
friendly	I like Kate. She's very **friendly**.
holiday	My friend is on **holiday** in Australia.
mask	My mum's carnival **mask** is very beautiful.
song	I love the **song** 'Royals' by Lorde.
stadium	I'm at the **stadium**. There's a football match today.
sweets	I like chocolate and **sweets**.
team	Mike is in our football **team**.
train	We're on the **train** with my mum.

Adjectives to describe feelings
SB page 22

1 ★ Unscramble the letters to make adjectives.

0 r e d i t   *t i r e d*

1 x c e t i e d   _ _ _ _ _ _ _

2 o r r w i e d   _ _ _ _ _ _ _

3 y a n g r   _ _ _ _ _

4 o r b e d   _ _ _ _ _

5 o h t   _ _ _

6 s t y i r t h   _ _ _ _ _ _ _

7 d a s   _ _ _

8 d l o c   _ _ _ _

9 g r y n u h   _ _ _ _ _ _

2 ★★ Complete the sentences with the adjectives in Exercise 1.

0 It's late and you're _____*tired*_____. Go to bed.

1 My new bike is broken. My dad's _____ with me.

2 I'm _____ . Let's play a game on your tablet.

3 My friends are _____ . There's a football match at our school today.

4 There's an exam at school today. Simon's _____ .

5 Andy's dog is ill. He's _____ .

6 I'm hot and _____ . Can I have a drink?

7 He's _____ . He wants a sandwich.

8 It's winter. It's _____ .

9 We're _____ . Let's go for a swim!

3 ★★★ (Circle) the correct adjectives.

0 A Are you *worried* / *excited* about the exam tomorrow?

   B No, I'm not. It's an easy exam.

1 A Is Kate *excited* / *bored* about the holiday?

   B Yes, she is.

2 A It's *cold* / *hot* today. Let's go for a swim.

   B Yes, OK. That's a good idea.

3 A Are you *hungry* / *thirsty*?

   B Yes, I am.

   A Let's have some pizza then.

4 A It's really *hot* / *cold* in here.

   B You're right. Let's close the window.

5 A I'm really *tired* / *thirsty*.

   B Here's a bottle of water.

   A Thanks.

6 A Mum's *angry* / *sad* with you.

   B Why?

   A You're late home.

Positive and negative adjectives
SB page 25

4 ★★ Unscramble the words and complete the sentences.

0 He's a _____*bad*_____ actor. (dba)

1 She's a _____ player. (ogod)

2 São Paulo is a _____ city. (arget)

3 The weather today _____ . (fluwa)

4 It's a _____ game. (unfyn)

5 There's an exam today. It's _____ ! (ritlerbe)

6 The pizzas here are _____ . (etnlcxele)

7 Volleyball is an _____ sport. (igecntix)

5 ★ Complete the sentences so they are true for you.

0 _____*Shakira*_____ is a great singer.

1 _____ is a good book.

2 _____ is a funny actor.

3 _____ is a terrible sport.

4 _____ is a great football player.

5 _____ is an exciting city.

6 _____ is an awful computer game.

7 _____ is a bad song.

8 _____ and _____ are excellent games.

6 ★★ Complete the dialogues so they are true for you. Use *Yes, I do* or *No, I don't* and an adjective from the list.

awful | bad | excellent | exciting
funny | good | ~~great~~ | terrible

0 A Do you like football?

   B _____*Yes, I do*_____ . It's a(n) _____*great*_____ sport.

1 A Do you like swimming?

   B _____ . It's a(n) _____ sport.

2 A Do you like the Harry Potter books?

   B _____ . They're _____ books.

3 A Do you like basketball?

   B _____ . It's a(n) _____ game.

4 A Do you like Ronaldo?

   B _____ . He's a(n) _____ football player.

5 A Do you like *The Hobbit* films?

   B _____ . They're _____ films.

Pronunciation
Vowel sounds – adjectives

Go to page 118.

READING

1 **REMEMBER AND CHECK** Complete the sentences with *likes* or *doesn't like*. Then look at the dialogue on page 24 of the Student's Book and check your answers.

0 Nick ___*doesn't like*___ Formula One.

1 Connor _____ Ben Stiller.

2 Nick _____ him.

3 Nick _____ One Direction.

4 Nick _____ ice cream.

5 Nick _____ Jenny Carter.

2 Read the profile of a famous singer quickly. Find and <u>underline</u> the answers to these questions.

1 What's her real name?

2 What's her stage name?

Name: Ella Yelich-O'Connor
Stage Name: Lorde
Nationality: New Zealander
Place of Birth: New Zealand
Likes: photography, music and books

The year is 2013. Ella Yelich-O'Connor is at secondary school. She's a sixteen-year old teenager from New Zealand. Her mother's name is Sonja Yelich and she's Croatian. Her father's name is Vic O'Connor and he's Irish. Ella is a famous singer, and her hit 'Royals' is at the top of the New Zealand charts. Her first album is in the top five in the UK, Canada, the USA, Ireland and Norway. Maybe it's a hit in your country, too! Ella Yelich-O'Connor is a queen of pop. She likes electronic music and she really likes hip hop.

She's a style icon but does she like fashion?
Yes, she does. She loves clothes.

Does she like social media?
Yes, she does. She likes Twitter and Instagram.

What does she like?
Ella likes books – all kinds of books. Books are important to her. The words of her songs are from books and her songs are like short stories.

3 Read the profile again and write short answers to the questions.

0 Is her stage name Ella? ___*No, it isn't.*___

1 Does she like photography? _____

2 Is Lorde from New York? _____

3 Is her father Irish? _____

4 Is she a singer? _____

5 Does she like electronic music? _____

6 Does she like clothes? _____

7 Are books important to her? _____

8 Is she popular in your country? _____

DEVELOPING WRITING

A text message

1 Read the text messages and <u>underline</u> the adjectives.

a

Hi, Amy. Are you still bored? Read a book! My favourite book is *Anne of Green Gables*. It's a great story. I really like Anne. She's friendly and funny. It's a happy story ☺. Please read it.
Kate

b

Hi, Matt. I'm at the cinema. The film is terrible. I don't like it. The actors are very bad. I don't like them. I'm really bored ☹. Where are you? Text me.
Tim

c

Hi, James. Are you at home? Listen to this song. It's great. The singer is excellent. The guitarist is good. I really like the song. Do you like it? Text me.
Lara

d

Hi, Sally. Thank you for the film. It's very funny. I really like it. My sister likes it too.
Jim Carrey is great. He's a very funny actor. The other actors are good, too. Speak soon.
Hannah

e

Hi, Tony. The song is terrible. The singer is awful. How is it number 1? I don't like it. My friends don't like it. Do you like it?
Jake

2 Write the adjectives in Exercise 1 in the correct columns.

Positive	Negative
	bored

3 Look at the text messages in Exercise 1. Use *likes* or *doesn't like* to complete the sentences.

0   Kate ___*likes*___ the book. It's a ___*happy*___ story.

1   Tim _____ the film. It's _____ .

2   Lara _____ the song. It's _____ .

3   Hannah _____ the film. It's _____ .

4   Jake _____ the song. It's _____ .

4 You like a book and you want to text a friend about it. Complete the text message.

Hi, _____ . Are you still bored? Read a book! My favourite book is _____ . It's a _____ story. I really like _____ . He/She is _____ . It's a _____ story. Please read it.

5 You don't like a film and you want to text a friend about it. Complete the text message.

Hi, _____ . I'm at the cinema. The film is _____ . I _____ it. The actors are _____ . I _____ them. I'm really _____ ☹. Where are you? Text me.

6 Think about a film, a book, a band or a song and write notes about it.

Title: _____
like / don't like   great / terrible
_____
_____
_____

Writing tip: Some useful language

I *like / don't like* the film.
I really *like / love* the film.
The *film / book / band / song* is *funny / exciting / sad*.
The *actor(s) / singer(s)* *is / are great / terrible / awful*.
The ending is *happy / sad*.

7 Now write a short text message about the film, book, band or song. Write 35–50 words.

LISTENING

1 🔊 15 **Listen to the dialogues. Which dialogue (1–5) matches the photo?**

2 🔊 15 **Listen again and mark the sentences T (true) or F (false).**

1	It's Emma's birthday.	T
2	Tom is cold.	
3	John doesn't like English.	
4	Tim doesn't like the film.	
5	Helen's cat is ill.	

3 🔊 15 **Listen again and circle the correct options.**

1 A Hi, Jane.
   B Oh, hi, Kate.
   A It's Emma's birthday today. Is she *happy /* *excited*?
   B Yes, she is. I'm *happy / excited*, too.

2 A What's the matter?
   B It's *hot / cold* in here. Are you *hot / cold*, Tom?
   A *No, I'm not. / Yes, I am.* I'm wearing a jumper.
   B Well, I'm very *hot / cold*. Can you *open / close* the window?
   A OK.

3 A There's an exam tomorrow. Are you worried, John?
   B No, I'm not worried about it. I *like / don't like* English. I'm just tired.
   A Well, I'm worried. I'm very worried. I *like / don't like* English.

4 A What's wrong, Tim? Are you *tired / bored*?
   B No, I'm not. I'm just *tired / bored*. I don't like this film.
   A Why? I *like / don't like* it. It's very funny.

5 A What's the matter with Helen? Why is she *sad / angry*?
   B Her cat's ill. It's at the vet.
   A Oh, no. That's *sad / terrible*. Poor Helen.

DIALOGUE

1 **Complete the dialogue with the words in the list.**

don't like | funny | great | ~~likes~~
likes | terrible

A Do you like the song 'Let it Go' from the film *Frozen*?

B No, I don't. But my little sister ⁰_____*likes*_____ it. It's her favourite song. She sings it all the time. In fact, she ¹_____ all the songs to the film.

A Do you like the film?

B No, I don't. It's ²_____ . I ³_____ animation films.

A Ah, I really like it. It's a ⁴_____ film. It's ⁵_____ .

▰▰ TRAIN TO THiNK ▰▰

Categorising

1 **Put the words in the list into categories. There are four words for each category.**

beach | Brazil | ~~cold~~ | New Zealand | sad
school | ~~stadium~~ | ~~the USA~~ | theatre
thirsty | tired | Turkey

Countries	Feelings	Places
the USA	*cold*	*stadium*

2 **Put words in these three categories.**

Nationalities	Colours	Classroom things

3 **Name the categories.**

1	2	3
good	fourteen	Lara
great	sixty-three	Tim
terrible	one hundred	Katy

EXAM SKILLS: Reading

Skimming

> ### Reading tip
>
> - Read the questions first. Then read the text quickly.
> - Think about what type of text it is. Is it a newspaper article? A letter or an email? A text message?
> - Underline the 'important' words, such as adjectives, nouns and verbs.
> - Try to answer *Wh-* questions – *Who, What, When* and *Where.*

1 Skim the text in Exercise 4. What type is it?

   A a newspaper article

   B an email

   C a text message

2 Find and write these 'important' words from the text.

two emotions

_____

_____

two positive adjectives

_____

_____

two negative adjectives

_____

_____

3 Complete the table with information about the text.

Who?	
What?	
When?	
Where?	

4 Read the text again and choose the correct answers (A or B).

> − □ ✕   ◀ ▶ 🏠
>
> Hi, Tess,
>
> I'm bored. It's my little brother Tim's birthday today. He's eight. He's very excited. All his friends are here. It's hot and sunny. They're in the garden now. His friends from his school football team are here. So of course, they all like football. His favourite team is Chelsea. I like Chelsea, too. They're an excellent team.
>
> Guess what his present from me is? It's a Chelsea football! Oh, and a book – *Henry Hunter and the Beast of Snagon*. It's a great story and I really like the pictures. They're excellent.
>
> His presents from Mum and Dad are a bike and a DVD. It's a really good bike but the film is terrible. It's called *Dumb and Dumber*. I don't like it. It isn't funny ☹.
>
> It's 11 am – Tim's birthday lunch is in an hour. But I'm hungry now. There's a big birthday cake ☺.
>
> See you soon,
>
> Samantha

0 Is Samantha excited?

   A Yes, she is.

   (B) No, she isn't.

1 Is it her brother's birthday today?

   A Yes, it is.

   B No, it isn't.

2 Is it a hot day?

   A Yes, it is.

   B No, it isn't.

3 Samantha _____ Chelsea.

   A likes

   B doesn't like

4 *Henry Hunter and the Beast of Snagon* is a/an _____ book.

   A awful

   B great

5 Samantha doesn't like the *Dumb and Dumber* films. They _____ funny.

   A are

   B aren't

6 Is Samantha thirsty?

   A Yes, she is.

   B No, she isn't.

CONSOLIDATION

LISTENING

1 🔊 16 **Listen to Annie and** (circle) **the correct answers (A, B or C).**

1 Annie is from …

A

the USA

B

South Africa

C

Mexico

2 She's …

A 12. B 13. C 14.

3 Her best friend is from …

A

Brazil

B

South Africa

C

the UK

4 Her best friend is called …

A Paulo.
B Pedro.
C Marcel.

2 🔊 16 **Listen again and mark the sentences T (true) or F (false).**

1 Annie is from Cape Town. ☐

2 She doesn't like sport. ☐

3 Her favourite athlete is a tennis player. ☐

4 Her favourite singer is Taylor Swift. ☐

5 Her best friend is Spanish. ☐

6 Her best friend is the same age as her. ☐

VOCABULARY

3 **Complete the sentences with the words in the list. There are two extra words.**

angry | exciting | expensive | fast | hungry | Japan
Japanese | old | Russian | terrible | thirsty | tired

1 Piano lessons aren't cheap. They're _____ .

2 Yuka is from Japan. She's _____ .

3 Dmitri is from Moscow. He's _____ .

4 The car isn't _____ . It's very slow.

5 My phone is _____ . It isn't new.

6 Dad is _____ . He isn't happy.

7 It's very late. I'm very _____ . Good night.

8 Water? Yes, please. I'm really _____ .

9 The new Bond film is really good. It's so _____ !

10 The Italian restaurant is bad. The food is _____ .

GRAMMAR

4 **Complete the dialogues with the missing words.**

1 A Do [0] _____*you*_____ like ice cream?
   B Yes, I love [1]_____ .

2 A [2]_____ you like dogs?
   B No, I don't like [3]_____ .

3 A Do you like Lucy?
   B Yes, I like [4]_____ . [5]_____ is my best friend.

4 A Do you like Mr Henderson?
   B No, I don't like [6]_____ . [7]_____ 's boring.

5 **Complete the sentences with the correct form of to be. Use contracted forms.**

0 I _*'m not*_ (✗) Spanish. I _*'m*_ Portuguese.

1 I _____ (✗) ten years old. I _____ eleven.

2 A _____ David happy?
   B No, he _____ .

3 Henry and Sally _____ from Australia.

4 A _____ you hungry?
   B Yes, we _____ .

5 Maria _____ (✗) twelve. She _____ eleven.

6 A Why _____ you angry?
   B Because you _____ late.

7 A How old _____ they?
   B Kevin _____ five and Sally _____ eight.

8 A Where _____ Ella from?
   B She _____ from South Africa.

DIALOGUE

6 Put the dialogue in order

	IZZY	I'm great. It's my birthday today.
	IZZY	I know. I'm really excited.
	IZZY	Bye.
	IZZY	Thanks. I'm off to the new pizza restaurant.
1	IZZY	Hi, Simon, how's it going?
	SIMON	Well, have fun. See you later.
	SIMON	That is so awesome! Happy Birthday!
	SIMON	Oh, hi, Izzy. I'm fine. How about you?
	SIMON	The new pizza restaurant? It's great.

READING

7 Read the text and complete the information in the form.

Personal information

Name: ⁰ *Brad Armstrong*

Age: ¹ _____

Nationality: ² _____

Likes: ³ _____

Favourite athlete: ⁴ _____

Favourite singer: ⁵ _____

Best friend: ⁶ _____

My name is Brad Armstrong. I'm 13 years old.
I'm from the USA. I live in Dallas.
I really like sport. I like basketball and football. My
favourite athlete is Tim Howard. He's a football player.
He's a goalkeeper and he's great.
I also like music. My favourite singer is Ed Sheeran.
He's a British singer. He's really good.
My best friend is Lisa. She's 13 and she's in my school.

8 Read the text again and correct the sentences.

0 Brad is from the UK.
  Brad is from the USA.

1 Brad's home town is Chicago.
  _____

2 Brad really likes rugby.
  _____

3 Tim Howard is a tennis player.
  _____

4 Brad's favourite singer is a woman.
  _____

5 Brad's best friend is a boy.
  _____

6 Lisa is 12.
  _____

7 Lisa isn't in his school.
  _____

WRITING

9 Write a short text about you. Use the questions to help you. Write 35–50 words.

- What is your name?
- How old are you?
- Where you are from and what is your nationality?
- What do you like?
- Who is your favourite athlete?
- Who is your favourite singer?
- Who is your best friend?

3 | ME AND MY FAMILY

GRAMMAR

Possessive 's `SB page 32`

1 ★★☆ Follow the lines and complete the sentences. Use 's.

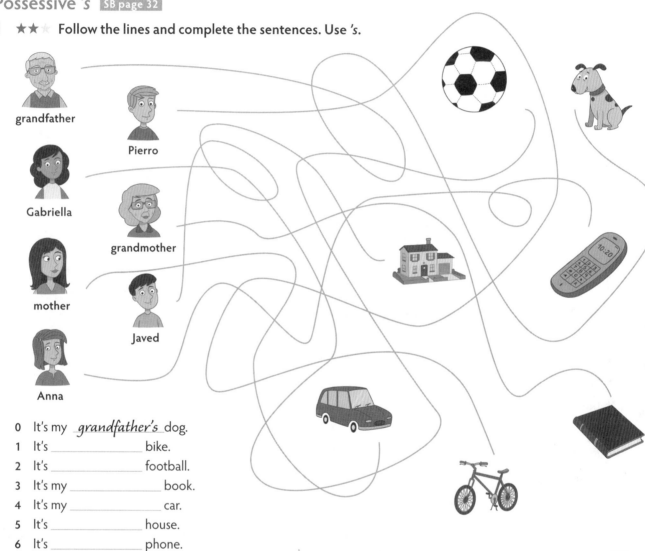

grandfather

Pierro

Gabriella

grandmother

mother

Javed

Anna

0 It's my _grandfather's_ dog.
1 It's _____ bike.
2 It's _____ football.
3 It's my _____ book.
4 It's my _____ car.
5 It's _____ house.
6 It's _____ phone.

Possessive adjectives `SB page 33`

2 ★☆☆ Complete the table.

	Possessive adjective
I	my
you	
he	
she	
we	
they	

3 ★★☆ Jake and Sally are at a birthday party. Circle the correct possessive adjectives.

JAKE Hi! What's ¹*your / his* name?

SALLY Sally.

JAKE Is that girl ²*her / your* friend?

SALLY Well, no. That's ³*my / their* sister. ⁴*His / Her* name's Marie. This is ⁵*our / your* house.

JAKE Oh. And those two boys?

SALLY They're ⁶*your / my* brothers. They're twins. They're twelve today. It's ⁷*their / our* birthday party. Wait a minute. Who are you?

JAKE I'm Jake. I'm with Mark. I'm ⁸*her / his* cousin.

SALLY Oh, right.

4 ★★   Complete the sentences.

0 It's George's dog. It's _____*his*_____ dog.
1 It's my mother's book. It's _____ book.
2 They're Jenny's sweets. They're _____ sweets.
3 It's Penny and Kate's apartment. It's _____ apartment.
4 It's my brother's and my TV. It's _____ TV.
5 They're John's CDs. They're _____ CDs.
6 It's my grandfather's chair. It's _____ chair.
7 I have three cousins – that's _____ house.
8 That's my family's car. It's _____ car.
9 A Is that _____ phone on the table?
   B No, this is _____ phone in my hand.
10 A Is _____ name Nina?
   B No, _____ name is Lara.

this / that / these / those   `SB page 34`

5 ★★   (Circle) the correct answers (A, B or C).

0 _____ is my bedroom.
   (A) This   B These   C Those
1 _____ is my new MP3 player.
   A Those   B That   C These
2 _____ are photos of my cat.
   A That   B These   C This
3 _____ computer on the table is my sister's.
   A Those   B These   C That
4 Are _____ your books over there?
   A these   B that   C those
5 Is _____ a good film?
   A these   B this   C those
6 _____ boys are from Brazil.
   A This   B That   C Those
7 _____ hotel is very expensive.
   A That   B Those   C These
8 _____ computer here is really slow.
   A That   B This   C These
9 Are _____ football players British?
   A this   B these   C that
10 Is _____ his pen?
   A these   B those   C this

6 ★★   Complete the sentences with *this*, *that*, *these* or *those*.

0 ____*These*____ are the books I want, here.
1 _____ are my friends, over there.
2 _____ is my new phone, just here.
3 _____ are my new CDs, here.
4 _____ is my father, over there.
5 _____ is my bed, right here.
6 _____ are my cousins, there.
7 _____ is my brother's laptop, right there.
8 _____ are my DVDs, here.

GET IT RIGHT! ◉

this and *these*

We use *this* to talk about singular objects that are near to us.
We use *these* to talk about plural objects that are near to us.

✓ **This** is my favourite dress.
✗ *These* is my favourite dress.
✓ **These** are my CDs.
✗ *This* are my CDs

Complete the sentences with *this* or *these*.

0 He gave me ____*this*____ shirt.
1 Is _____ your pencil?
2 _____ are my favourite sweets.
3 I got _____ book yesterday.
4 Are _____ your computer games?
5 _____ are my old trainers.
6 I like _____ photo.

Pronunciation

this / that / these / those

Go to page 118.

VOCABULARY

Family members

MALE	FEMALE
son	daughter
father	mother
brother	sister
grandfather	grandmother
uncle	aunt
husband	wife
grandson	granddaughter
cousin	cousin

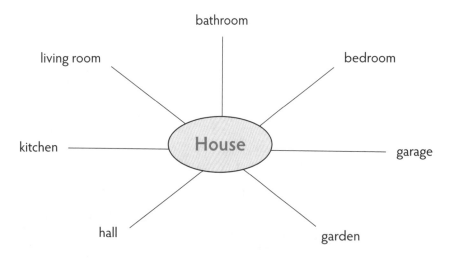

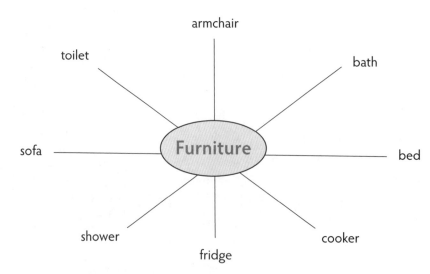

Key words in context

apartment   We live in an **apartment** on the 6th floor.

curtains   In my bedroom, there are green **curtains** on the window.

home   The house is very small, but it's my **home** and I love it.

photograph   I take great **photographs** with my new camera.

princess   She's the daughter of the king, so she's a **princess**.

queen   The UK and Denmark both have a **queen**.

Family members SB page 32

1 ★ Complete the words.

0 au *n t*

1 _ o _

2 _ o _ _ e _

3 _ u _ _ a _ _

4 _ i _ e

5 _ o u _ i _

6 _ _ a _ _ o _ _ e _

7 _ _ a _ _ a _ e

8 _ _ a _ _ o _

2 ★★ Complete the puzzle. What's the mystery word?

```
1 [ ][O][ ][ ][ ]
  2 [ ][ ][T][ ]
    3 [ ][S][ ][ ][ ]
      4 [ ][H][ ][ ]
  5 [ ][ ][E][ ]
  6 [ ][ ][E][ ]
    7 [ ][ ][G][ ][ ][ ]
```

1 My _____ is forty-five; she's a teacher.

2 My _____ Julie is my mother's sister.

3 My little _____ is only five years old.

4 I'm twelve and my _____ is fourteen.

5 My _____ is from London. He's English.

6 My _____ Paolo is from Brazil.

7 Our teacher's _____ is in our class.

3 ★★★ Write answers to the questions so they are true for you.

1 Is your family big or small?

_____

2 What are your parents' names?

_____

3 How many cousins have you got?

_____

4 How many aunts and uncles have you got?

_____

5 Where do the people in your family live?

_____

6 How many people do you live with?

_____

House and furniture SB page 35

4 ★ Circle the odd one out in each list.

0	bath	shower	(sofa)
1	armchair	bedroom	kitchen
2	shower	hall	bathroom
3	cooker	bed	fridge
4	bedroom	garage	living room
5	garage	kitchen	garden
6	toilet	hall	kitchen

5 ★★ Look at photos 1–5. Where in a house are these things? Write the words.

0 *living room* _____

1 _____

2 _____

3 _____

4 _____

5 _____

6 ★★★ Are these things in the correct place? Mark ✓ (yes, OK), ? (maybe) or ✗ (no).

1 a shower in the garden ☐

2 a sofa in the bedroom ☐

3 a car in the garage ☐

4 a fridge in the bedroom ☐

5 a cooker in the garage ☐

6 a car in the hall ☐

7 a toilet in the bathroom ☐

8 an armchair in the garden ☐

READING

1 **REMEMBER AND CHECK** Mark the sentences T (true) or F (false). Then look at the article on page 31 of the Student's Book and check your answers.

0 Kate Middleton is English. `T`

1 She likes playing football. ☐

2 Kate's family is from Scotland. ☐

3 She has a sister called Elizabeth. ☐

4 Kate is very famous now. ☐

5 William's grandfather is Prince Charles. ☐

6 She has a daughter called Ann. ☐

7 Kate's home is a small house. ☐

2 Read the blog quickly. Is Mary Ann's family big or small?

My family and I

Hi, everybody! This is the first post on my blog. I'm Mary Ann. I'm fourteen and I live in London. I have two brothers. Mark is twelve and Stephen is sixteen. My father is a teacher, but not at my school. Mum is from Canada and she works in London. She's a photographer for a newspaper.

I have a grandfather and grandmother in London and lots of aunts, uncles and cousins here, too. My mother's family are in Canada – her parents and her brother and sister. So I have family there, too. My favourite aunt is Polly. She's great and she's always nice to me. She's my father's sister.

Our house isn't big, but I have my own small bedroom. It's my favourite room in the house. I have photos and posters in my room and I have a table for my laptop and two chairs, and a bed, of course. Mark and Stephen's bedroom is big with two beds and a TV. They have a table and a shelf for their books and DVDs.

We also have a dog called Sport. He's Mark's pet. He's very big.
I have a cat. Her name is Smokey. She's my favourite.

Well, that's it for today. Please add your comments and questions.

3 Read the blog again and complete the sentences with words from the text.

0 Mary Ann has two __brothers__ , Mark and Stephen.

1 Her father is a _____ .

2 Her mother is from _____ .

3 She's a _____ .

4 Mary Ann has family in _____ and in _____ .

5 Mary Ann's favourite aunt is called _____ .

6 Mary Ann's favourite room is her _____ .

7 Her brothers have two _____ and a TV in their room.

DEVELOPING WRITING

My bedroom

1 Read the text. Find three or more differences between Jake's perfect bedroom and his real bedroom.

My perfect bedroom and my real bedroom

My perfect bedroom is big. The walls are yellow and the floor is brown. The bed is very big – it's 2 metres long and 1.6 metres wide (I like big beds!). It's very comfortable, too, and it's the colour that my favourite football team plays in. So it's black and white because my favourite team is Juventus. The desk is near the window, with a comfortable chair for me to sit and work on my great new computer.

My real bedroom isn't big. The floor is brown but the walls are blue. The bed is OK but it isn't very big and it isn't very comfortable! The bed is black and white – yay! My desk is near the door and the chair is small but it's OK. And I like my computer. It's old but it's really good!

---

2 Complete the sentences with *and* or *but*.

0 The walls are yellow ____*and*____ the floor is brown.

1 The bed is big _____ it's comfortable.

2 The bed is comfortable _____ it's in Real Madrid colours, too.

3 The computer is old _____ it's really good.

3 Think about your perfect bedroom and about your real bedroom. Use the ideas below to help you make notes.

	My real bedroom	My perfect bedroom
big / small?		
wall colour?		
floor colour?		
big / small bed?		
comfortable?		
bed colour?		
near the window?		
chair?		

4 Use your notes to write about your real bedroom and your perfect bedroom.

My real bedroom

My real bedroom _____ big. The floor is _____ and the walls are _____ . The bed is _____ . The bed is _____ . The _____ is near the window. The chair is _____ .

My perfect bedroom

My perfect bedroom _____ big. The floor is _____ and the walls are _____ . The bed is _____ . The bed is _____ . The _____ is near the window. The chair is _____ .

LISTENING

1 🔊 **18** Listen to the dialogue and complete the sentences. Write *Tony*, *Christine* or *Jack*.

0   *Christine*   says the room is nice.

1 _____ is Tony's brother.

2 _____ likes watching football.

3 _____ loves films.

4 The CDs are _____'s.

2 🔊 **18** Listen again and complete the words in this part of the dialogue.

CHRISTINE   Wow! Are these your DVDs, Tony?
They're [0]g *reat*_____ !
I [1]l_____ films.

TONY   No, they're my brother's. He really
[2]l_____ old films. Very, very old films.

CHRISTINE   [3]W_____ a [4]n_____
collection!

TONY   Yeah. It's not bad. But the films are a bit
boring!

CHRISTINE   No, they're great! Hey! Are these your CDs?
They're [5]f_____! This one
[6]i_____ really [7]c_____!

TONY   Yeah, I [8]r_____ [9]l_____ Ella
Henderson. She's my favourite. She's a great
singer.

CHRISTINE   Let's listen to it now!

TONY   OK.

DIALOGUE

1 Put the dialogues in order.

Dialogue 1

[ ] LUCY   Yes, it is cool. I love T-shirts!

[1] LUCY   Happy birthday, Pat! This is a present for
you.

[ ] LUCY   This one? It's from Italy. It's a birthday
present from my Italian friend.

[ ] PAT   For me? Thanks, Lucy! Oh, a T-shirt! And it's
really cool!

[ ] PAT   Your T-shirt's nice, too. I really like it.

Dialogue 2

[ ] ALLY   Is your brother there, too?

[ ] ALLY   Hi, Jim. Thanks. Wow, I really like your house.

[ ] JIM   Thank you! Come into the kitchen. My mum
and dad are there.

[1] JIM   Hi, Ally! Nice to see you. Come in!

[ ] JIM   No, he's not. He's in his bedroom.

2 Look at Exercise 1 and complete the dialogues between you and a friend.

Dialogue 1

YOU   I really [1]*like* / *love* your T-shirt. Is it new?

FRIEND   Yes, it's from [2]_____ .

YOU   It looks [3]*great* / *nice* / *fantastic*.

FRIEND   Thanks.

Dialogue 2

YOU   What a [4]*nice* / *great* / *fantastic* CD!

FRIEND   Yes, it's by [5]_____ .

YOU   I really [6]*like* / *love* it.

FRIEND   Let's listen to it now.

Dialogue 3

YOU   What a [7]*fantastic* / *good* / *great*
computer game!

FRIEND   Yes. It's called [8]_____ .

YOU   I really [9]*love* / *like* computer games.

FRIEND   OK. Let's play it together!

3 Now write your own dialogue.

PHRASES FOR FLUENCY

SB page 37

1 ★ ☆ ☆ Complete the phrases with the missing vowels.

0   R e a lly?

1   __h, r __ght.

2   L __t's g __.

3   J __st __ m __n __t __.

2 Complete the dialogue with the phrases in the list.

just a minute | let's go | oh, right | ~~really~~

ANA   That boy over there is really nice.

JO   [0]__*Really*__ ? Him? Well, he isn't my
favourite person.

ANA   I think he looks really cool.

JO   Well, he is, but sometimes he's difficult.

ANA   Hey, [1]_____ . Isn't he in your
family?

JO   Yes, he's my brother.

ANA   [2]_____ . Your brother. OK.

JO   Ana, [3]_____ ! We're late for class!

Sum it up

1 Look at the pictures and complete the crossword.

ACROSS

1
6
7
8
9

DOWN

2
3
4
5
8

2 Read the website about a famous house. Which of the things in the house is impossible to have?

Upton Abbey

Come and visit Upton Abbey! This famous house is 400 years old. The Hogworth family live here – Lord Hogworth, Lady Hogworth and their four children.

Walk in the gardens! Walk round the house and visit its 20 bedrooms! And the 400-year-old kitchen – it's wonderful.

See ten fantastic old cars in the garage. See the 300-year-old fridge in the kitchen. See the old baths in the bathrooms. Everything here is old and different!

Open every weekend, 10.00–17.00, Friday, Saturday and Sunday. Only £10.00 per person or £25.00 for a family of three or more.

3 Complete the page from the website with information from the text.

- ⁰Age of house   *400 years old*
- ¹Family name   _____
- ²Number of bedrooms   _____
- ³Age of kitchen   _____
- ⁴Number of cars   _____

- ⁵Opening time   _____
- ⁶Closing time   _____
- ⁷Days open   _____
- ⁸Price per person   _____
- ⁹Price for a family (3+) _____

4 | IN THE CITY

GRAMMAR

there is / there are `SB page 40`

1 ★ ☆ ☆ **Complete the sentences with *is* or *are*.**

0   There _____are_____ four bedrooms in the house.

1   There _____ two Brazilian girls at our school.

2   There _____ lots of famous squares in Paris.

3   There _____ a mountain near Tokyo called Mount Fuji.

4   _____ there a desk in your bedroom?

5   There _____ a small fridge in my parents' bedroom.

6   There _____ nine or ten big train stations in London.

7   There _____ eight people in my family.

8   _____ there any good shops here?

2 ★ ★ ☆ **Complete the text with *there is*, *there isn't*, *there are* or *there aren't*.**

Alice is 14. Here is what she says about Rosewood, her local shopping centre.

'I really like our local shopping centre. It's small, but ⁰ _there is_ a cinema. ¹ _____ some cafés on the top floor, but ² _____ any restaurants. My mum likes it because ³ _____ two good bookshops and ⁴ _____ a great supermarket. My sister likes it because ⁵ _____ some cool clothes shops. My brother doesn't like it because ⁶ _____ a good sports shop (and he loves sport!). My dad doesn't like shopping.'

some / any `SB page 40`

3 ★ ☆ ☆ (Circle) **the correct options.**

0   There are (some) / any books in my room.

1   There aren't *some* / *any* good shops here.

2   There are *some* / *any* nice curtains in their house.

3   There aren't *some* / *any* interesting books in the library.

4   There aren't *some* / *any* banks in this street.

5   There are *some* / *any* fantastic things in the museum.

6   There aren't *some* / *any* cafés in the park.

7   There are *some* / *any* supermarkets in the town centre.

8   There are *some* / *any* chairs in the garden.

4 ★ ★ ☆ **Complete the sentences with *some* or *any*.**

0   There are _____some_____ good shops.

1   There aren't _____ sports shops.

2   There aren't _____ cinemas.

3   There are _____ computer shops.

4   There aren't _____ phone shops.

5   There are _____ cafés.

5 ★ ★ ☆ **Complete the text with *there is a*, *there isn't a*, *there are some* or *there aren't any*.**

Tim is 12. This is what he thinks of Parkland, his local shopping centre.

'The shopping centre near my house is really big. There are about 400 shops in it. ⁰ _There is a_ fantastic food hall. ¹ _____ café with great ice creams. I like it because ² _____ good cinemas and a library, too. Mum says ³ _____ good shoe shops, but they're not my favourite places. ⁴ _____ DVD shop and ⁵ _____ great music shops. The only bad things are that ⁶ _____ computer shops and ⁷ _____ restaurant.'

6 ★★★ Complete the questions with *Is there a* or *Are there any*. Then look at the texts in Exercises 2 and 5 and answer the questions. Use *Yes, there is/are.*, *No, there isn't/aren't.* or *I don't know.*

0   *Is there a* _____ supermarket in Rosewood?
    Yes, there is.

1   _____ cinemas in Rosewood?

2   _____ computer shop in Rosewood?

3   _____ clothes shops in Rosewood?

4   _____ sports shops in Rosewood?

5   _____ bank in Parkland?

6   _____ café in Parkland?

7   _____ library in Parkland?

8   _____ music shops in Parkland?

9   _____ restaurant in Parkland?

7 ★★★ Complete these sentences about a shopping centre you know.

1   There are _____ .

2   There aren't _____ .

3   There aren't _____ .

4   There are _____ .

5   There is _____ .

6   There isn't _____ .

Imperatives SB page 41

8 ★ Circle the correct options.

0   OK, everyone. Please *listen* / *don't listen* to me. This is important.

1   Are you tired? *Go* / *Don't go* to bed late tonight.

2   Please *be* / *don't be* quiet in the library.

3   It's cold in here. *Open* / *Don't open* the window, please.

4   Hello. Please come in and *sit* / *don't sit* down.

5   Wow! *Look* / *Don't look* at that fantastic statue.

6   It's a very expensive shop! *Buy* / *Don't buy* your new clothes there!

7   To get to the cinema, *turn* / *don't turn* left at the supermarket, and it's there.

8   *Listen* / *Don't listen* to your brother. He's wrong.

9 ★★ Mick and Josh are looking for a sports shop. Complete the dialogue with the words in the list.

go | listen to | look | open | ~~sit down~~ | turn

MICK   Where's the sports shop?

JOSH   OK, [0] *sit down* on this chair and [1] _____ at the map.

MICK   I haven't got a map.

JOSH   Oh, well I've got an app.

MICK   Well [2] _____ the app on your phone, then.

JOSH   OK, OK. Wait a minute. Oh! Look, there's the sports shop. [3] _____ down here and [4] _____ left. The sports shop is behind the chemist's.

MICK   Is it opposite the phone shop?

JOSH   No, [5] _____ me again, Mick! It's on the corner, behind the chemist's.

GET IT RIGHT!

some and *any*

We use *some* in affirmative sentences and *any* in negative sentences.

✓ I've got **some** time.

✗ I've got ~~any~~ time.

✓ He hasn't got **any** money.

✗ He hasn't got ~~some~~ money.

Complete the sentences with *some* or *any*.

0   I haven't got _____ *any* _____ pets.

1   There are _____ good games.

2   Don't bring _____ food.

3   They haven't got _____ homework.

4   I have _____ time.

5   I have _____ presents for you.

6   We don't have _____ problems.

VOCABULARY

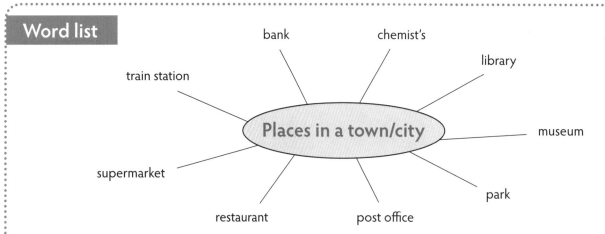

Places in a town/city

- bank
- chemist's
- library
- train station
- museum
- supermarket
- park
- restaurant
- post office

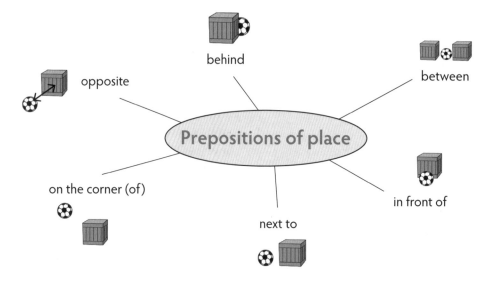

Prepositions of place

- behind
- between
- opposite
- in front of
- on the corner (of)
- next to

Numbers

one hundred and thirty	130
one hundred and fifty	150
one hundred and seventy-five	175
two hundred	200
five hundred and sixty	560
one thousand	1,000
one thousand two hundred	1,200
two thousand	2,000

Prices

dollar	$
pound	£
euro	€
nine pounds and ninety-nine	£9.99
twenty-one dollars and ninety-five cents	$21.95
seventy-two euros and fifty cents	€72.50

Key words in context

bookshop	This is a great **bookshop**. They've got books in different languages here.
expensive	That shirt is £150.00; it's very **expensive**!
famous	The Eiffel Tower in Paris is very **famous**.
palace	The king and queen live in that **palace**. It's got twenty bedrooms!
shoe shop	There's a new **shoe shop** in town. Their shoes are really nice!
square	St Peter's **Square** in Rome is very famous.
statue	There's a **statue** of a famous woman here.
tower	The BT **Tower** in London is 191 metres tall!

Places in a town/city SB page 40

1 ★★   **Where are these people? Write a word from the list.**

bank | chemist's | library | museum
park | ~~post office~~ | restaurant
supermarket | train station

0   Hi. This letter to Australia, please.
     post office

1   Six apples and some bananas, please.
     _____

2   Look! These things are 200 years old!
     _____

3   A return ticket to Cambridge, please.
     _____

4   Please be quiet in here. People are reading.
     _____

5   It's a great day for a picnic here.
     _____

6   Hi. Can I change these dollars for pounds, please?
     _____

7   The steak and salad for me, please.
     _____

8   I need some medicine for my eye.
     _____

Prepositions of place SB page 41

2 ★   **Look at the map of the shopping centre and (circle) the correct options.**

0   The computer shop is *behind /* (*next to*) the bank.
1   The computer shop is *between / in front of* the bank and the bookshop.
2   The bookshop is *opposite / on the corner.*
3   The shoe shop is *between / opposite* the supermarket.
4   The bank is *next to / behind* the shoe shop.
5   The café is *behind / in front of* the cinema.

Pronunciation

Word stress in numbers
Go to page 119. 🔊

3 ★★   **Use the prepositions in Exercise 2 to complete the sentences.**

0   The chemist's is ___next to___ the supermarket.
1   The restaurant is _____ the shoe shop.
2   The post office is _____ the restaurant and the phone shop.
3   The restaurant is _____ the supermarket.
4   The sports shop is _____ the chemist's.
5   The cinema is _____ the café.
6   The phone shop is _____ the bookshop.

Numbers 100+ SB page 42

4 ★   **Write the words or numbers.**

0   110   _one hundred and ten_
1   _____   one hundred and seventeen
2   125   _____
3   _____   one hundred and ninety-eight
4   215   _____
5   _____   three hundred and twelve
6   652   _____
7   _____   one thousand three hundred
8   1,400   _____
9   _____   two thousand six hundred and twenty

Prices SB page 43

5 ★★   **Write the prices in words.**

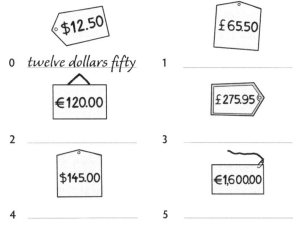

0   _twelve dollars fifty_   1   _____

2   _____   3   _____

4   _____   5   _____

6 ★★★   **Write the name of places/things you know.**

1   a famous tower   _____
2   a good shoe shop   _____
3   a famous square   _____
4   a statue of a famous person   _____
5   a famous palace   _____

READING

1 REMEMBER AND CHECK (Circle) the correct options. Then look at the brochure on page 39 of the Student's Book and check your answers.

0 Shenzhen is a (city)/ river.

1 Window of the World is in *China / Japan.*

2 It's a *museum / park.*

3 There are models of famous places from around *China / the world.*

4 You can take a ride on the *Hudson / Colorado* river.

5 China's national day is *January 1st / October 1st.*

6 There is a festival of *Chinese / pop* music every year.

7 There *are some / aren't any* restaurants in the park.

2 Read the emails quickly. Who lives in Australia?

From: Jack M
To: HarryP@mail.com
Subject: New home

Hi, Harry!

How are things in Sydney? Is it warm and sunny there? We're on holiday now and it's very cold and wet here in England. Nothing new there! December isn't my favourite month. There's some football on TV, but there are a lot of programmes about cooking and people dancing. There's a new café in town, but it's between a museum and the library. There are always a lot of old ladies in it – no young people.

I'm bored! Please email and tell me about Australia.

Jack

From: Harry P
To: JackM@mail.com
Subject: Re: New home

Hi, Jack!

Thanks for your email. I love it here. We're on holiday, too, but we're still in Sydney. And yes, it's very hot and sunny. There are some great beaches and lots of things to do. Our apartment isn't in the centre of town; it's opposite the beach! Sydney is fantastic. There are great cinemas and theatres, parks and, of course, Sydney Harbour Bridge and the famous Opera House. The bridge is beautiful, but opera isn't my favourite music. There are lots of great places to eat and some really cool cafés. My mum loves all the shopping centres.

Next email, all about my new school!!!!

Harry

---

3 Read the emails again. Mark the sentences T (true) or F (false).

0 It's December. `T`

1 Harry and Jack are on holiday. ☐

2 There's a new shoe shop in Jack's town. ☐

3 Jack loves the new café. ☐

4 Harry lives in a house. ☐

5 There are lots of cinemas in Sydney. ☐

6 Harry's favourite music is opera. ☐

7 Harry's mum likes the shopping centres. ☐

8 Harry is at a new school. ☐

DEVELOPING WRITING

Your town/city

1 **Read the text. Does the writer like weekends in her town?**

A weekend in my town

I like my town. It isn't very big but the people here are nice.

At the weekend, there are lots of things to do. The town centre is small but there are some nice shops and cafés, so I go into the centre on Saturday morning to meet my friends. We have coffee or a sandwich together, or we do some shopping. Some days we don't buy anything, but it's always fun.

There's a cinema in the town too, so on Saturday night or Sunday afternoon, my friends and I see a film together. I like football, so on Sunday morning I play with lots of friends in the park. There are three football pitches in the park. It's really good.

Not far from the town centre there is a river. It's great to swim there, but only in the summer!

My town is OK and my friends are great, so the weekends here are not bad.

2 **Complete the sentences with *or, and* or *so*.**

1 On Saturday evening we go to the cinema _____ we see a film.

2 Do you want to play football _____ volleyball?

3 My cousins live 300 kilometres away, _____ I don't visit them very often.

3 **Match the words 1–3 with the phrases a–c.**

1 in ☐

2 on ☐

3 at ☐

a the weekend

b the summer

c Sunday afternoon

4 **Think about a weekend in your town/city. What do you do? Use the ideas below to help you make notes.**

What I do on Saturday _____

_____

What I do on Sunday _____

_____

What I do with my friends _____

_____

What we do in summer _____

_____

What we do in winter _____

5 **Use your notes to complete the text.**

Weekends in my town/city

I live in _____ . I _____ my town/city.
_____ the weekend I _____
Saturday morning. _____ Saturday afternoon I
_____ . On Sunday I _____ . With my
friends I _____ . _____ the summer
we _____ but _____ the winter we
_____ .

LISTENING

1 🔊20 **Listen to Stella and Matthew talking to their Aunt Mary. Tick (✓) the places they talk about.**

bank	☐
bookshop	☐
café	☐
chemist's	☐
library	☐
museum	✓
park	☐
post office	☐
shopping centre	☐
station	☐
supermarket	☐

2 🔊20 **Listen again and correct the sentences.**

0 There isn't a good shopping centre.
   There's a good shopping centre.

1 The museum is on Grand Parade.
   _____

2 The museum is very big.
   _____

3 The shopping centre is next to the museum.
   _____

4 Stella wants some pens and pencils for her project.
   _____

5 There aren't any cafés in the shopping centre.
   _____

6 Aunt Mary's favourite café is next to the bookshop.
   _____

DIALOGUE

1 **Stella is in a clothes shop. Put the dialogue in order.**

☐	WOMAN	£15.50.
☐	WOMAN	OK. That's £31.00, please.
1	WOMAN	Hello. Can I help you?
☐	WOMAN	Yes. There's this one here.
☐	STELLA	Hi. Yes. Have you got any yellow T-shirts?
☐	STELLA	Great! I'll take two, please.
☐	STELLA	Oh, it's really nice. How much is it?

2 **Complete the dialogue with the words and phrases in the list.**

~~Can~~ | expensive | is | much | That's | three

MAN   ⁰ ___*Can*___ I help you?

MATTHEW   Yes, have you got any maps of the town?

MAN   Yes, there are ¹_____ different maps.

MATTHEW   How ²_____ are they?

MAN   They're £1.50 each.

MATTHEW   OK, three, please.

MAN   That's £4.50.

MATTHEW   And how much ³_____ that small book about the museum?

MAN   It's £5.70.

MATTHEW   And that big book?

MAN   That's £25.00.

MATTHEW   That's very ⁴_____ . Just the maps and the small book.

MAN   OK. ⁵_____ £10.20.

3 **Imagine you're in a bookshop. Write a dialogue similar to the one in Exercise 1.**

_____
_____
_____
_____
_____
_____
_____
_____
_____
_____

▓▓ TRAIN TO THiNK ▓▓

Exploring numbers

Seth and John have to buy things for their room at home. They have £300. They buy five things and they have £35 left. Tick (✓) what they buy.

armchair – £60	☐
bed – £50	☐
chair – £20	☐
desk – £30	☐
DVD player – £25	☐
table – £35	☐
TV – £100	☐

Identifying text type

1 🔊 **21** Listen to people talking in three different situations. How many people are speaking?

Situation 1: _____

Situation 2: _____

Situation 3: _____

2 Match the descriptions with the pictures. Write 1–3 in the boxes.

1 a news report on TV

2 an announcement at a train station

3 people in a shop

3 🔊 **21** Listen again. Match the situations with the pictures.

Situation 1 → picture ☐

Situation 2 → picture ☐

Situation 3 → picture ☐

Listening tip

**When you listen to a text for the first time, you don't need to understand every word.
Listen to the important things:**

● Number of speakers.

● Sounds and noises to tell you where the speakers are.

● The way the speakers talk, e.g. are they happy, angry, worried, sad, excited, bored or none of these?

● 'Important' words – read the question first and think of words (nouns, adjectives or verbs) that might help you to answer it. These are 'important' words to listen for.

4 🔊 **21** Listen again to the three situations. Which words helped you in Exercise 3?

Situation 1: _____

Situation 2: _____

Situation 3: _____

CONSOLIDATION

LISTENING

1 🔊 **22** Listen to Jeff talking about his family and where they live. (Circle) the correct answers (A, B or C).

1 How many people are there in Jeff's family?

   A six   **B** eight   **C** ten

2 How many sisters has Jeff got?

   A four   **B** five   **C** six

3 Where is Jeff from?

   A the USA **B** the UK   **C** Canada

4 What's his cousin called?

   A Paul   **B** Brad   **C** Clint

2 🔊 **22** Listen again. How many are there? Write the numbers in the boxes.

A

B

C

D

E

F

VOCABULARY

3 Match the words in A with the words in B to make pairs.

A

~~bathroom~~	uncle
living room	brother
son	kitchen
garage	husband

B

car	daughter
sofa	cooker
wife	sister
~~shower~~	aunt

0 *bathroom — shower*

1 _____

2 _____

3 _____

4 _____

5 _____

6 _____

7 _____

4 Name the shops and write the prices.

0 £3.29

   chemist's — It's three pounds twenty-nine.

$14.99

1 _____

£2.50

2 _____

€79.59

3 _____

£12.99

4 _____

GRAMMAR

5 **Complete the sentences with the words in the list. There are two extra words.**

any | her | his | is | some | their | those | turn

1 Ask Luke. It's _____ sandwich.
2 There _____ a big park near my house.
3 Paul is Danny and Olivia's brother. He's _____ brother.
4 The shoe shop? OK, just _____ right on the High Street and it's there.
5 There aren't _____ parks near here.
6 Can I see _____ trousers in the window, please?

DIALOGUE

6 **Complete the dialogue.**

JORDAN   I like your T-shirt, Rachel.
RACHEL   [1]R _____ ? It's very old.
JORDAN   Well I think it [2]l_____ cool. And [3]w_____ a great hat, too.
RACHEL   [4]T_____ you. It's new.
JORDAN   How [5]m_____ was it?
RACHEL   Well, it was a present from my mum.
JORDAN   Oh, [6]r_____ . I'll ask her then.

READING

7 **Read the dialogue and complete the sentences.**

WOMAN   Hello, can I help you?
JEFF   Yes, I'd like to see those T-shirts behind you.
WOMAN   These red ones?
JEFF   No, the blues ones next to them.
WOMAN   OK. Yes, these are really nice. Here you are.
JEFF   How much are they?
WOMAN   Wait a minute. Let me see. They're £9.99.
JEFF   OK, can I have three, please?
WOMAN   Wow. You really like them.
JEFF   They're not for me. They're for my sisters.
WOMAN   Sisters?
JEFF   Yes. It's their birthday tomorrow.
WOMAN   So they're triplets?
JEFF   Yes, all three born on the same day.
WOMAN   Is it difficult? I mean having three sisters?
JEFF   Three! There's two more as well.
WOMAN   Five sisters! Poor you. Here, have another T-shirt for you.
JEFF   Wow, thanks. That's really kind.

1 Jeff wants to see the _____ T-shirts.
2 The T-shirts are _____ each.
3 The T-shirts are for his _____ .
4 It's their _____ tomorrow.
5 Triplets are _____ children born on the same day.
6 Jeff has _____ sisters.
7 The woman gives Jeff a free _____ .
8 Jeff thinks the woman is very _____ .

WRITING

8 **Write a short text about your family and where you live. Write 35–50 words. Use the questions to help you.**

- Who is there in your family?
- What is your house like?
- What is your town like?

5 IN MY FREE TIME

GRAMMAR

Present simple SB page 50

1 ★☆☆ **(Circle)** the correct options.

0 I **(play)** / plays tennis every day.

1 My brothers *speak* / *speaks* Spanish.

2 Mr Jones *teach* / *teaches* Maths.

3 The dog *like* / *likes* the park.

4 We sometimes *go* / *goes* to bed very late.

5 You *live* / *lives* near me.

2 ★★☆ **Complete the sentences with the present simple form of the verbs in brackets. Which four sentences match with the pictures? Write the numbers in the boxes.**

0 My dad ___*flies*___ planes. (fly)

1 The boys _____ a lot of video games. (play)

2 Miss Dawes _____ English. (teach)

3 Suzie _____ in the library every day. (study)

4 Tim and Dana _____ the guitar. (play)

5 Mum _____ flowers. (love)

A

B

C

D

3 ★★☆ **Complete the sentences with the correct form of the verbs in the list.**

finish | go | ~~like~~ | play | speak | study | teach | watch

0 Mum ___*likes*___ pop music.

1 My father _____ Music at my school.

2 Lucy _____ to a Glee club on Wednesdays.

3 Sam _____ four languages. He's amazing.

4 My brother _____ TV on Saturday mornings.

5 Our school _____ at 3.15 pm.

6 Gordon _____ the piano every day after school.

7 My sister _____ at a school in Birmingham.

Pronunciation

Present simple verbs – 3rd person

Go to page 119. 🔊

Adverbs of frequency SB page 50

4 ★☆☆ **Put the adverbs in the correct order.**

☐ often **1** always ☐ sometimes ☐ never

5 ★★☆ **Write the sentences with the adverb of frequency in the correct place.**

0 I meet my friends in town on Saturdays. (sometimes)

   I sometimes meet my friends in town on Saturdays.

1 Jennie is happy. (always)

   _____

2 They do homework at the weekend. (never)

   _____

3 You help Dad make dinner. (sometimes)

   _____

4 We are tired on Friday afternoons. (often)

   _____

5 It rains on Saturdays! (always)

   _____

6 Mum flies to New York for work. (often)

   _____

7 I am bored in English lessons. (never)

   _____

6 ★★★ **Write sentences so they are true for you. Use adverbs of frequency.**

1 do homework after school

_____

2 play sport at the weekend

_____

3 watch TV on Sunday mornings

_____

4 listen to music in the morning

_____

5 phone my best friend in the evening

_____

Present simple (negative) SB page 51

7 ★★ **Complete the sentences with the negative form of the verbs in brackets.**

0 My mum _doesn't write_ books for children. (write)

1 I _____ to football lessons after school. (go)

2 My cousins _____ to a lot of music. (listen)

3 My dad _____ model planes. (make)

4 We _____ games on our tablet. (play)

5 School _____ at 8.15 am. (start)

6 My sister _____ singing or dancing. (like)

7 You _____ in a small house. (live)

8 ★★ **Match these sentences with the sentences in Exercise 7.**

0	0	She writes for teenagers.
a		It's really big.
b		But the gates open at that time.
c		We play them on the computer.
d		She's quite shy.
e		I go to them on Saturdays.
f		He makes trains.
g		But they watch a lot of TV.

Present simple (questions) SB page 52

9 ★ **Complete the questions with do or does.**

0 _Do_ you live in Manchester?

1 _____ Paul like sport?

2 _____ you know the answer?

3 _____ your sister play the piano?

4 _____ you often go to the cinema?

5 _____ your teacher give you a lot of homework?

10 **Write the questions. Then write answers to the questions so they are true for you.**

0 your mother / speak English?

Does your mother speak English?
Yes, she does.

1 you / always do your homework?

_____

_____

2 your best friend / play tennis?

_____

_____

3 you / sometimes play computer games before school?

_____

_____

4 you and your friends / play football?

_____

_____

5 your mum / drive a car?

_____

_____

GET IT RIGHT! ◉
Adverbs of frequency

With the verb *be*, we use this word order: subject + verb + adverb of frequency.

With other verbs, we use this word order: subject + adverb of frequency + verb.

✓ **He is always** friendly.

✗ ~~He always is friendly.~~

✓ **I often watch** football on TV.

✗ ~~I watch often football on TV.~~

(Circle) **the correct sentences.**

0 a I eat often pizza.
 (b) I often eat pizza.

1 a I go out often with friends.
 b I often go out with friends.

2 a I always go to the cinema with my friends.
 b Always I go to the cinema with my friends.

3 a Music is always great.
 b Music always is great.

4 a I play football in the park never.
 b I never play football in the park.

5 a I sometimes am bored.
 b I am sometimes bored.

VOCABULARY

Free-time activities

play computer games

dance

hang out with friends

go shopping

do homework

chat with friends online

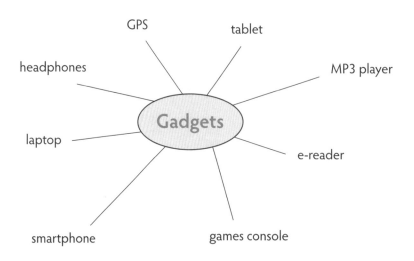

GPS · tablet · headphones · MP3 player · laptop · **Gadgets** · e-reader · smartphone · games console

Days of the week

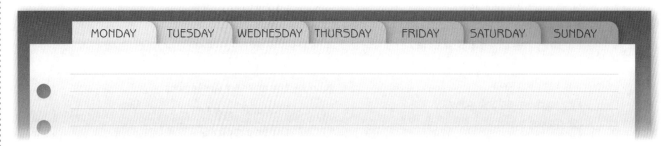

MONDAY TUESDAY WEDNESDAY THURSDAY FRIDAY SATURDAY SUNDAY

Key words in context

carry	Don't **carry** all those books. They're very heavy.
cheer	I always **cheer** when my team scores a goal.
concert	I often go to pop **concerts** at the O2 stadium.
feel	I **feel** tired. I want to go to bed.
finish	School **finishes** at 4 pm.
fly	My mum **flies** planes for British Airways.
help	Dad often **helps** me with my homework.
meet	I sometimes **meet** my friends in the park at the weekend.
perform	My school **performs** a play every year.
sing	My dad always **sings** in the shower.
study	I **study** at St George's school.
teach	Mr O'Brian **teaches** Maths.

Free-time activities SB page 50

1 ★ ☆ ☆ **Match the parts of the sentences.**

0	I play	e
1	I go	☐
2	I hang out with	☐
3	I do	☐
4	I listen to	☐
5	I dance	☐

a shopping with Dad on Saturdays.

b my homework when I get home.

c music in my bed.

d to rock music in my bedroom.

e computer games on my tablet.

f my friends in the park on Sundays.

2 ★★ ☆ **Complete the sentences with the words in the list.**

dance | his homework | listens | out
plays | shopping

0 Every day after school I hang _____*out*_____ at the park.

1 Lucy goes _____ with her sister on Saturday mornings.

2 Tim never does _____ on time.

3 We _____ every weekend at the disco.

4 My brother _____ computer games all weekend!

5 My dad _____ to really old music!

3 ★★★ **Write sentences that are true for you. Use adverbs of frequency.**

1 play computer games

_____

2 go shopping

_____

3 dance

_____

4 do homework

_____

5 listen to music

_____

6 hang out with friends

_____

7 do sport

_____

8 go to the cinema

_____

Gadgets SB page 53

4 ★★ ☆ **Unscramble the letters to make words for gadgets.**

0	blteat	*tablet*
1	megas loscone	_____
2	P3M replay	_____
3	marsthopen	_____
4	ahehndspoe	_____
5	SGP	_____
6	plapto	_____
7	arae-der	_____

5 ★★★ **Answer the questions so they are true for you.**

1 Q What do you use to play computer games?

A _____

2 Q What do you use to listen to music?

A _____

3 Q What do you use to find your way?

A _____

4 Q What do you use to read books, magazines or articles?

A _____

Days of the week SB page 53

6 ★★ ☆ **Complete the days of the week with the missing letters. Then put the days in order.**

1	M o nday
☐	_ _ dnesday
☐	_ _ iday
☐	_ _ esday
☐	_ _ nday
☐	_ _ ursday
☐	_ _ turday

7 ★★★ **Choose three days. Write sentences so they are true for you.**

I love Fridays because I always go to the
cinema with my dad in the evening.

_____

_____

_____

_____

_____

READING

1 REMEMBER AND CHECK Complete the sentences with the missing words. Then look at the newsletter on page 49 of the Student's Book and check your answers.

0   The text is about a school _Glee_____ club.

1   People s_____ at these clubs.

2   Miss Higgins is a M_____ teacher.

3   They sing songs from f_____ .

4   They perform c_____ in front of the rest of the school three times a year.

5   The club is a good way to make f_____ .

6   The club is in the school h_____ .

7   They meet on Tuesdays and F_____ .

2 Look at the pictures and read the messages opposite. What rooms are these people in? What club are they in?

1   _____
    _____

2   _____
    _____

3   _____
    _____

4   _____
    _____

3 Match the sentences with the correct places (A–D) in the messages.

0   Tell your parents it finishes at 5 pm.   [C]

1   (and some old songs, too).   [ ]

2   It's great for all students who love gadgets. [ ]

3   Ask your parents about some of their favourites, and we can add them to the list. [ ]

Computer gaming club

Come and get better at all your favourite games. Learn from your friends and show them what you know. Mrs Stephens also shows you how to make your own simple games.

A _____

Years 7 and 8 – Tuesday lunchtime in Room 4

• Dance club •

Join Mr Roberts for an hour of exercise and have loads of fun at the same time. Learn how to dance to all the best modern pop songs B_____ And it's not just for students at the school – anyone is welcome!'

All years – Wednesday lunchtime in the school gym

Homework club

Don't do all of your homework after school or at weekends. Come to Homework club and do it before you go home. When you get home after school you can have fun! C_____ There's always a teacher here to help you if you have a problem.

All years – Every day after school in Room 8

Film club

Watch classic films from the 1980s and 1990s *E.T., Toy Story, Jurassic Park* etc. Then talk about them with Miss Owens and other students. D_____ Bring your own popcorn!

Years 9–11, Thursday after school in Room 14

DEVELOPING WRITING

My week

1 Read the text. On which day does Bruno not do any homework?

POSTED: MONDAY 10 APRIL

Bruno's Busy Life

A typical week …

From Monday to Friday, I go to school from 9 am to 3 pm every day. But my day doesn't finish then!

After school on Mondays I have piano lessons from 4 pm to 5 pm. In the evenings I do my homework.

On Tuesdays and Thursdays I go to Tennis club from 4 pm to 6 pm. In the evenings I do my homework.

On Wednesday afternoons I go to Dance club from 3 pm to 4 pm. And in the evenings? Yep, I do my homework.

On Fridays I do my homework after school! I go to Glee club in the evenings. It finishes at 9 pm.

On Saturdays I do things with Mum and Dad. We go shopping or visit Grandma. My dad sometimes takes me to watch the football.

On Sundays I sleep! Oh, and then I do some homework.

2 Complete the sentences with the correct prepositions. Use the text in Exercise 1 to help you.

1   I play tennis _____ Tuesdays and Thursdays. I play _____ 4 pm _____ 6 pm.

2   _____ Wednesday afternoons I go to Dance club. It starts _____ 3 pm and finishes _____ 4 pm.

3   _____ Monday to Friday I go to school.

3 Match the parts of the phrases. Then check your answers in the text in Exercise 1.

1   do ▢
2   go ▢
3   have ▢

a   a tennis lesson
b   to Dance club / shopping
c   homework

4 Think about your life. Use the questions to make notes about the things you do.

What do you do in the day?

_____

What do you do in the evening?

_____

What do you do at the weekend?

_____

5 Use your notes to complete the text so it is true for you.

A typical week …

From Monday to Friday I go to school. _____ every day! But my day doesn't finish then.

After school on Mondays I _____ .
In the evenings _____ .
On Tuesdays _____ .
In the evenings _____ .
On Wednesdays _____ .
In the evenings _____ .
On Thursdays _____ .
In the evenings _____ .
On Fridays _____ .
In the evenings _____ .
On Saturdays _____ .
On Sundays _____ .

LISTENING

1 🔊24 **Listen and put the events in order.**

- ▢ **a** Jane feels better.
- ▢ **b** Jane tells her mum about the singing.
- ▢ **c** Jane tells her mum the name of the song.
- ▢ **d** Jane tells her mum the name of the play.
- ▢ *1* **e** Jane is unhappy.
- ▢ **f** Mum starts playing the piano.

2 🔊24 **Listen again and correct the sentences.**

0 Jane is in the school tennis team.

Jane is in the school play.

1 Jane likes acting and singing.

_____

2 Jane thinks she's a good singer.

_____

3 The song is from *The Lion King*.

_____

4 Mum is a good piano player.

_____

DIALOGUE

1 **Complete the dialogue with the phrases in the list.**

don't worry | here to help you | No problem
You can do this | ~~You're good~~

JANE	Yes, my character is Elsa! She sings a lot in the play. And I'm a terrible singer.
MUM	You aren't. ⁰ _You're good_ . Just like me.
JANE	Really?
MUM	Yes, really. Come on. ¹_____ .
JANE	I can?
MUM	Yes, you can. And I'm ²_____ .
JANE	You are?
MUM	Yes, ³_____ . Now what's the song?
JANE	It's `Let it Go' from the film.
MUM	⁴_____ . Come with me to the piano.

2 **Look at the picture and write a short dialogue. Use phrases from Exercise 1.**

PHRASES FOR FLUENCY SB page 55

1 **Match the sentences.**

- **0** What's wrong? ▢ *d*
- **1** I've got an idea. ▢
- **2** Ana, do you want to be in the school tennis team? ▢
- **3** I don't want to play football. ▢

- **a** Really. What is it?
- **b** No way!
- **c** Oh, come on. We really need you.
- **d** I feel a bit ill.

2 **Use two of the pairs of sentences in Exercise 1 to complete the dialogues.**

Dialogue 1

GEORGE _____

SARA _____

GEORGE But I hate football. And I'm terrible at it.

SARA No, you're not. You're great.

Dialogue 2

ABI I'm sorry, Simon. I don't really want to go shopping.

SIMON _____

ABI _____

SIMON Oh, dear. Let me get you a glass of water.

3 **Use the other two pairs of sentences in Exercise 1 to make your own dialogues.**

Sum it up

1 This is Lucy's diary. Make sentences about her week.

0 *On Monday she goes shopping.*

1 _____

2 _____

3 _____

4 _____

5 _____

MONDAY	shopping
TUESDAY	dance
WEDNESDAY	friends
THURSDAY	computer games
FRIDAY	homework
SATURDAY	music
SUNDAY	sleep!

2 Use the code to work out the message.

CODE

♋ = a	♌ = b	♍ = c	♎ = d
♏ = e	♐ = f	♑ = g	♒ = h
⅄ = i	♈ = j	& = k	● = l
○ = m	■ = n	□ = o	▢ = p
❑ = q	❒ = r	◆ = s	◆ = t
◆ = u	❖ = v	◆ = w	⊠ = x
▣ = y	⌘ = z		

3 What do you want? Use the code to write your own message.

_____

_____

6 FRIENDS

GRAMMAR

have / has got (positive and negative)
SB page 58

1 ★ ☆ ☆ (Circle) the correct options.

0 I *has got /* (*have got*) a new friend.

1 My friend, Sam, *has got / have got* a tablet.

2 Jenny *has got / have got* a big family.

3 We *has got / have got* a cat.

4 All of my friends *has got / have got* bikes.

2 ★★ ☆ Look at the table and complete the sentences.

has / hasn't got	Sally	Tom	Dan	Ellie
smartphone	✓	✗	✓	✗
laptop	✗	✗	✗	✗
bike	✓	✗	✓	✓
TV	✗	✓	✗	✗
dog	✓	✓	✓	✓

0 Tom _*hasn't got*_ a smartphone.

1 Sally _____ a laptop or a TV.

2 Dan and Ellie _____ a bike.

3 Tom _____ a TV.

4 All of them _____ a dog.

5 Tom and Dan _____ a laptop.

3 ★★★ Write sentences so they are true for you. Use *have got* or *haven't got* and the phrases in the list.

a big family | a new phone number
a new smartphone | a sister | a tablet
black hair | brown eyes | three brothers

1 _____

2 _____

3 _____

4 _____

5 _____

6 _____

7 _____

8 _____

4 ★★★ Write sentences under the pictures. Use the phrases in the list and *have got* or *has got*.

a shaved head | long curly hair
long straight hair | short curly hair

_____

have / has got (questions) SB page 59

5 ★ ☆ ☆ (Circle) the correct options.

1 A (*Have*) */ Has* you got a TV in your bedroom?

  B No, I *haven't / hasn't.* But my brother has got one.

2 A *Have / Has* Katy got a friendship band?

  B No, she *haven't / hasn't.* She doesn't like them.

3 A *Have / Has* Jake and Andy got new mobile phones?

  B No, they *haven't / hasn't.* But I *have / has* got one.

4 A *Have / Has* you got lots of songs on your mobile?

  B Yes, I *have / has.* I've got thousands. I listen to them all the time.

5 A *Have / Has* you got bikes?

  B Yes, we *have / has.* We've both got bikes. We ride to school every day.

6 A *Have / Has* Simon got a sister?

  B No, he *haven't / hasn't.* He's got a brother.

6 ★★ Complete the dialogue with the correct form of *have got*.

JANE   0 ___*Has*___ your mum ___*got*___ brown hair?

MARCUS   No, she 1 _____ . She 2 _____ black hair.

JANE   3 _____ she _____ blue eyes?

MARCUS   No, she 4 _____ . She 5 _____ green eyes.

JANE   6 _____ she _____ a daughter?

MARCUS   No, she 7 _____ . She 8 _____ one son – me!

7 ★★★ Complete the dialogue about a member of your family.

FRIEND   Has he/she got green eyes?

YOU   _____

FRIEND   Has he/she got a big family?

YOU   _____

FRIEND   Has he/she got a car?

YOU   _____

FRIEND   Has he/she got a dog?

YOU   _____

FRIEND   Has he/she got a smartphone?

YOU   _____

Countable and uncountable nouns
SB page 59

8 ★ Write C (countable) or U (uncountable).

0	chair	*C*	5	time	
1	nose		6	work	
2	hair		7	hospital	
3	fun		8	name	
4	friend		9	teacher	

9 ★★ (Circle) the correct options.

0 It's the weekend. Let's have *a* / (some) fun.

1 I've got *a* / *some* sandwiches. I'm hungry. Let's eat one.

2 Let's listen to *a* / *some* music on your smartphone.

3 Marie's got *a* / *some* red bike.

4 I've got *a* / *some* money. Let's buy an ice cream.

5 He's got *a* / *some* hobby – painting!

6 My dad's got *a* / *some* work to do.

7 Murat hasn't got *an* / *some* apple. He's got *a* / *some* banana.

10 ★★ Complete the dialogues with *a*, *an* or *some*.

1 A Would you like ___*some*___ ice cream?

   B No, thanks. I've got _____ apple.

2 A Have you got _____ hobby?

   B Yes, I have. I sing in a band.

3 A Have you got _____ best friend?

   B Yes, I have. Her name's Zeynep.

4 A I've got _____ money from my mum.

   B Me too!

   A That's good. Let's buy _____ sweets.

5 A I haven't got a pen.

   B Oh, I've got _____ . I've got blue, black and red. Is that OK?

   A Yes, perfect!

GET IT RIGHT!
Countable and uncountable nouns

We add *-s* to the end of countable nouns to make them plural, but not to uncountable nouns.

✓ *I have a lot of **friends**.*

✗ *I have a lot of friend.*

✓ *I drink a lot of **water**.*

✗ *I drink a lot of waters.*

(Circle) the correct options.

0 How many *pen* / (pens) has he got?

1 I listen to *musics* / *music* in my bedroom.

2 They have a lot of *hobby* / *hobbies*.

3 Do you have enough *money* / *moneys* for your lunch?

4 Homework isn't always a lot of *fun* / *funs*.

5 Her brother has two *phone* / *phones*.

6 This street has a lot of *shop* / *shops*.

VOCABULARY

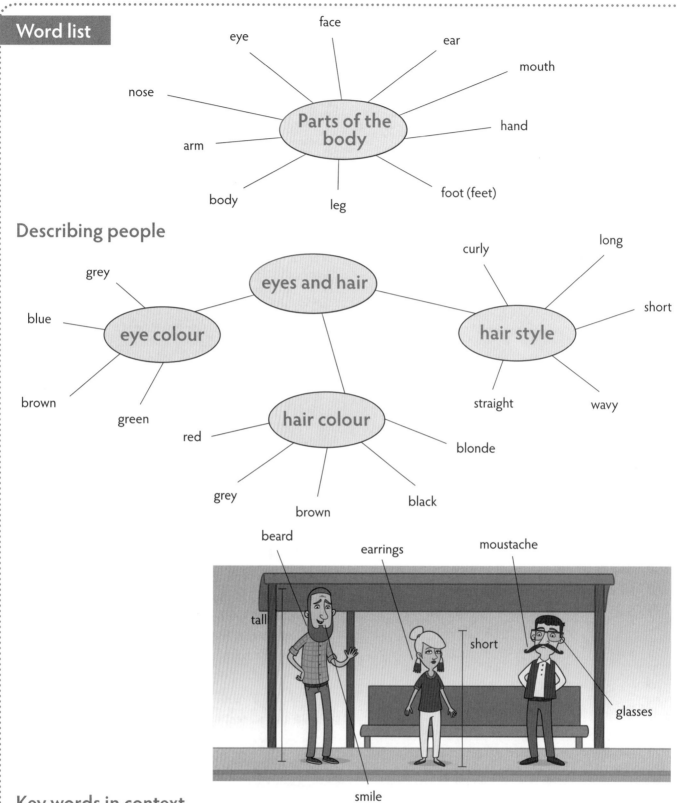

Parts of the body

- face
- eye
- ear
- mouth
- nose
- hand
- arm
- foot (feet)
- body
- leg

Describing people

eyes and hair

eye colour
- grey
- blue
- brown
- green

hair style
- curly
- long
- short
- straight
- wavy

hair colour
- red
- grey
- brown
- black
- blonde

- beard
- earrings
- moustache
- tall
- short
- glasses
- smile

Key words in context

doctor	When I'm ill, I see a **doctor**.
good-looking	James has got black hair and blue eyes. He's very **good-looking**.
kiss	When we greet a friend in my country, we **kiss** three times on the cheeks.
nurse	My mum is a **nurse** at a hospital.
shaved	My dad hasn't got any hair. He's got a **shaved** head.
surprise	I've got a present for Jane. It's a **surprise**.
tradition	I always eat cake on my birthday. It's a **tradition**.

Parts of the body `SB page 58`

1 ★ Complete the crossword.

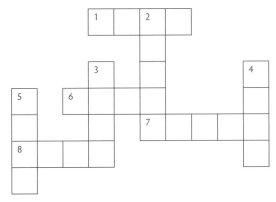

ACROSS

1 You reach with your _____ .
6 You kick with your _____ .
7 You hold with your _____ .
8 You hear with your _____ .

DOWN

2 You eat with your _____ .
3 You walk with your _____ .
4 You smell with your _____ .
5 You see with your _____ .

Describing people (1) `SB page 60`

2 ★★ (Circle) the correct options.

0 His hair isn't curly. It's (wavy) / brown.
1 She's got *short / blonde* red hair.
2 Her eyes are *straight / green*.
3 My mother always wears her hair *straight / brown* for work.
4 The old man has grey *curly / hair*.
5 His hair *colour / style* is black.

Describing people (2) `SB page 61`

3 ★ Complete the words with *a, e, i, o* or *u*.

0 m o u s t a c h e
1 g l _ s s _ s
2 t _ l l
3 b _ _ r d
4 s m _ l _
5 _ _ r r _ n g s
6 s h _ r t

4 ★★ Match the words to the pictures. Write 1–6 in the boxes.

1 beard | 2 earrings | 3 glasses | 4 grey
5 moustache | 6 wavy

5 ★★★ Look at the picture and write the names of the people.

0 She's got earrings. *Seline*
1 He's got a very big moustache. _____
2 She's got a lovely smile. _____
3 He's got a very long beard. _____
4 She wears glasses. _____

6 ★★★ Write one more sentence about each person in Exercise 4.

1 _____
2 _____
3 _____
4 _____

Pronunciation

Long vowel sound /eɪ/

Go to page 119.

READING

1 REMEMBER AND CHECK **Mark the sentences T (true) or F (false). Then look at the article on page 57 of the Student's Book and check your answers.**

0 Delaney Clements is 12. `F`

1 Delaney has got long curly hair and blue eyes. ☐

2 She loves sports. ☐

3 Kamryn is her best friend. ☐

4 Delaney has got cancer. ☐

5 Delaney shaves her head. ☐

2 **Read the two dialogues about friendship and answer the questions.**

1 Who has got green eyes? _____

2 Who wears glasses? _____

JANET	Who is your best friend?
CLARA	Sarah is my best friend.
JANET	What does she look like?
CLARA	She's very pretty. She's got long curly black hair and brown eyes. She wears glasses and she's got a friendly smile.
JANET	What's she like?
CLARA	She's very clever and she's very kind. She likes drawing and making things. I like making things, too. We've got the same hobbies. That's important, I think.
JANET	Why is she a good friend?
CLARA	Friends share things with you. Sarah shares everything with me. She shares her chocolate with me and her clothes with me. She's a very special friend.

JANET	Who is your best friend?
SAM	Murat is my best friend.
JANET	What does he look like?
SAM	He's tall and he's got short straight brown hair and green eyes. He's got a friendly smile and he laughs a lot. We laugh a lot together. We like the same things.
JANET	What's he like?
SAM	He's funny and tells good jokes. He's very good at sports, and he likes basketball. I like basketball, too. We like the same team. That's important, I think.
JANET	Why is he a good friend?
SAM	Friends listen to you. Murat always listens to me. Sometimes I have a problem and he helps me. He's a great friend.

3 **Read the dialogues again and answer the questions.**

1 What colour is Sarah's hair? _____

2 What colour is Murat's hair? _____

3 Who likes basketball? _____

4 Who likes drawing? _____

5 What do Murat and Sam like? _____

6 What does Sarah share with Clara? _____

4 **Who says these phrases about friendship? Write C (Clara) or S (Sam).**

A good friend …

1 ☐ shares things with you.

2 ☐ likes the same team.

3 ☐ helps you.

4 ☐ has the same hobbies.

5 ☐ tells you jokes.

6 ☐ listens to you.

DEVELOPING WRITING

Describing people in a story

1 Read about a singer from a story.
Mark the sentences T (true) or F (false).

1 He's short. ☐
2 He wears glasses. ☐
3 He's got a moustache. ☐
4 He hasn't got a beard. ☐
5 He doesn't like tennis. ☐

In my story, there's a singer. He's in a boy band. He's very tall. He's got short black hair and blue eyes and he wears glasses. He's got a short beard. I think he's very good-looking. He's very active. He likes football and swimming, but he doesn't like tennis. He's very friendly. Look! He's got a big smile. I think he's cool.

2 Think of a person from a story. He/She can be a singer, a sports person, an actor/actress, a prince/princess, etc. Choose the adjectives that describe him or her.

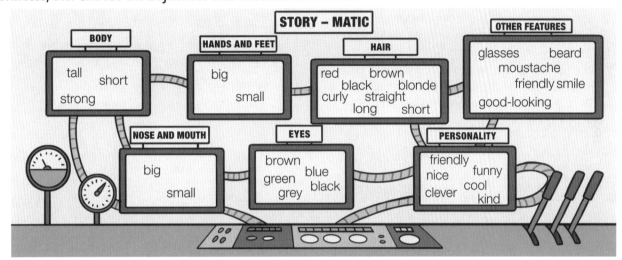

STORY – MATIC

BODY
tall short
strong

HANDS AND FEET
big
small

HAIR
red brown
black blonde
curly straight
long short

OTHER FEATURES
glasses beard
moustache
friendly smile
good-looking

NOSE AND MOUTH
big
small

EYES
brown
green blue
grey black

PERSONALITY
friendly
nice funny
clever cool
kind

3 Write notes about your story person. Use the questions to help you.

What does he/she look like? (hair, eyes, other features) _____

_____

Personality _____

_____

Likes/dislikes _____

_____

4 Use your notes to complete the text about
your story person.

In my story, there is a/an _____ .
He/She is _____ . He/She has got
_____ and _____ .
He/She has also got _____ and
_____ . And what about his/her
personality? He/She is _____
and _____ . He/She likes
_____ but he/she doesn't like
_____ .

I like him/her very much.

Writing tip: adjectives to describe people

● He/She is *tall / short*.
● He/She has got *long / black / curly* hair.
● He/She has got *brown / blue / green* eyes.
● He/She has got a *black / grey / brown / long / short moustache / beard*.
● He/She is *nice / friendly*.

LISTENING

1 🔊27 Listen to the dialogues and number the places in the order you hear them.

a ☐ the park

b ☐ a hospital

c ☐ a party

2 🔊27 Listen again and (circle) the correct options.

1 Martin is *tall* / *short* and he's got short curly *brown* / *black* hair. He's got a *moustache* / *friendship band* and he wears *glasses* / *earrings*.

2 Katie has got a *dog* / *bike* with her. She's *short* / *tall* and she's got long curly *brown* / *black* hair. She's got *brown* / *blue* eyes and she always wears *glasses* / *earrings*. She's very *funny* / *friendly*.

3 The nurse is *tall* / *short* and she's got *short* / *long* hair. It's *black* / *blonde* and it's *curly* / *straight*. She's got *brown* / *green* eyes and she's very *popular* / *pretty*.

DIALOGUE

1 Put the dialogue in order.

☐	POLICE OFFICER	And what's your daughter's name?
☐	POLICE OFFICER	And what colour eyes has she got?
1	POLICE OFFICER	Can I take your name?
☐	POLICE OFFICER	Thank you, Mrs Jones.
☐	POLICE OFFICER	OK, first, what colour hair has she got?
☐	POLICE OFFICER	Is it long or short?
☐	MRS. JONES	She's got brown hair.
☐	MRS. JONES	My name's Sarah Jones.
☐	MRS. JONES	She's got green eyes and she wears glasses.
☐	MRS. JONES	It's Emma.
☐	MRS. JONES	It's short and curly.

▰▰ TRAIN TO THiNK ▰▰

Attention to detail

Spot the five differences and write sentences.

Picture 1

Picture 2

0 *In picture 1, the man has got glasses.*
   In picture 2, he hasn't got glasses.

1 _____

  _____

2 _____

  _____

3 _____

  _____

4 _____

  _____

Punctuation (getting apostrophes right)

Writing tip

When writing in English, it's sometimes easy to make mistakes with apostrophes ('). It's important to know when to use them and when not to use them.

- We use apostrophes to show missing letters in short forms, for example:

  He is … → He's …

  She has got … → She's got …

- Be careful not to confuse apostrophes for the short form of *be* and *have got* with apostrophes to show possession:

  My mum's got curly hair. (short form)

  My mum's name is Helen. (possession)

1 Complete the *Apostrophe Challenge*. Write the short forms.

I think I can complete the *Apostrophe Challenge* in _____ seconds.

I am	**0**	*I'm*
It is	**1**	
You are	**2**	
He is not	**3**	
They are not	**4**	
She has got	**5**	
I have got	**6**	
We have got	**7**	
He has not got	**8**	
I have not got	**9**	

My time: _____ seconds.

2 Read the text. Put apostrophes in the correct places.

My best friends name is Miranda. Shes

12 years old and shes in the same class

as me. Mirandas got short curly brown

hair and green eyes. She wears glasses

and shes very pretty. Shes clever and she

likes sports. Mirandas got a brother and

a sister. Theyre eight years old and ten

years old. Theyve got brown hair and blue

eyes. They dont wear glasses. Mirandas

also got a cat. Its black and white and its

names Suky. Its a lovely cat.

3 Write a paragraph about one of these people. Use the questions in the box to help you.

a your best friend

b a family member

c your favourite actor/singer/band

- What's his/her name?
- How old is he/she?
- What does he/she look like?

CONSOLIDATION

LISTENING

1 🔊 **28** Listen to three dialogues and (circle) the correct answers (A, B or C).

1 Jonathan has got a problem with his …
   A arm.   B hand.   C leg.

2 Maddy is …
   A nice.   B short.   C tall.

3 How many friends has Tim got?
   A about fifty   B about fifteen   C about five

2 🔊 **28** Listen again and answer the questions.

1 What does Jonathan want to do today?

   _____

2 What does the girl tell him to do?

   _____

3 Does Mike know Maddy?

   _____

4 What does Mike want Samantha to say to Maddy?

   _____

5 When does Tim come to this place?

   _____

6 What colour is Steve's hair?

   _____

GRAMMAR

3 (Circle) the correct options.

TOM Hi Joanna. How are you? It's nice to see you here.

JOANNA Hi Tom. Well, I [1]*go always / always go* to the shopping centre on Saturdays.

JASON Oh, right. [2]*I'm never / I never am* in town on Saturdays. But it's different today because [3]*I've got / I'm got* some money.

JOANNA Great. [4]*How much / How many* money have you got, then?

TOM £75.00. I [5]*don't know / know not* what I want to buy, though. Maybe some clothes, or … .

JOANNA That's a great idea. I love clothes. I [6]*buy / buys* clothes every month.

TOM Really? So, [7]*you got / you've got* lots of clothes at home?

JOANNA Yes, that's right.

TOM OK, well I'm not very good at buying clothes. Can you help me? Have you got [8]*a / some* time to come with me?

JOANNA Of course. Let's go to this shop first – [9]*it's always got / it's got always* nice things to buy.

TOM OK, cool. You know, Joanna, it's great to have [10]*a / some* friend like you!

VOCABULARY

4 Complete the sentences with the words in the list. There are two extra words.

do | earrings | e-reader | eyes hang out | headphones | legs short | smile | tall

1 I really like listening to music with my _____ .

2 Spiders have got eight _____ .

3 I like Susannah. She's always happy and she's got a nice _____ .

4 These are my new _____ . Do you like them?

5 I don't buy books any more. I've got an _____ .

6 She's good at basketball because she's very _____ .

7 I only _____ my homework on Sundays – never on Saturdays!

8 On Sundays I always _____ with my friends.

5 Complete the words.

1 My favourite day of the week is F _ _ _ _ _ _ .

2 I use my new t _ _ _ _ _ every day to check my emails and things.

3 Her hair isn't straight. It's c _ _ _ _ _ .

4 Let's go out on W _ _ _ _ _ _ _ _ evening – to the cinema, maybe?

5 My grandfather's got a b _ _ _ _ and a moustache.

6 His eyes aren't very good. He wears g _ _ _ _ _ _ _ all the time.

7 Do you want to go s _ _ _ _ _ _ _ in town tomorrow morning?

8 Put your h _ _ _ _ up if you know the answer.

DIALOGUE

6 **Complete the dialogue with the words in the list.**

always | an idea | haven't got | listen to | never | on | play | tablet | way | wrong

PAUL   Hey, Jenny. You don't seem very happy. What's ¹_____ ?

JENNY   Hi, Paul. I'm OK. It's nothing.

PAUL   Come ²_____ . Tell me. Is there a problem?

JENNY   No, not really. I want to ³_____ computer games tonight, but I ⁴_____ anyone to play with.

PAUL   OK. Listen. I've got ⁵_____ . Let's ask James to come over to my place. Then we can all play some games together.

JENNY   No ⁶_____ ! I don't like James at all. He ⁷_____ helps me or says anything nice to me. He's ⁸_____ horrible to me.

PAUL   Oh, right, OK. So – let's play, you and me. I'm not very good, but …

JENNY   Oh, yes, please. That's great, Paul. Thank you. So – can we use your laptop?

PAUL   Sorry, Jenny, I haven't got a laptop. But I've got a ⁹_____ . Is that OK?

JENNY   Yes, I think so. And we can ¹⁰_____ music at the same time, too.

PAUL   Sure. OK, let's go.

READING

7 **Read this text about gadgets and (circle) the correct answers (A or B).**

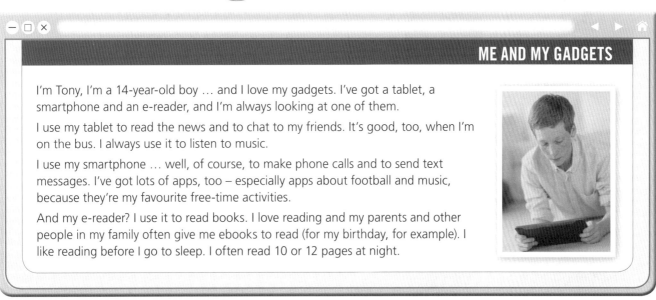

ME AND MY GADGETS

I'm Tony, I'm a 14-year-old boy … and I love my gadgets. I've got a tablet, a smartphone and an e-reader, and I'm always looking at one of them.

I use my tablet to read the news and to chat to my friends. It's good, too, when I'm on the bus. I always use it to listen to music.

I use my smartphone … well, of course, to make phone calls and to send text messages. I've got lots of apps, too – especially apps about football and music, because they're my favourite free-time activities.

And my e-reader? I use it to read books. I love reading and my parents and other people in my family often give me ebooks to read (for my birthday, for example). I like reading before I go to sleep. I often read 10 or 12 pages at night.

1 Tony's got …
   A three gadgets.
   B four gadgets.

2 He listens to music on …
   A his smartphone.
   B his tablet.

3 Tony uses his smartphone to …
   A read about the news and weather.
   B talk to his friends.

4 People in Tony's family often give him …
   A ebooks for his reader.
   B pages from books to read at night.

WRITING

8 **Write a paragraph about your gadgets. Use the questions to help you. Write 35–50 words.**
   ● What gadgets have you got?
   ● What do you use them for?
   ● When / How often do you use them?
   ● What gadgets do you want?

7 SPORTING LIFE

GRAMMAR

can (ability) SB page 68

1 ★☆☆ Match the sentences with the pictures. Write 1–8 in the boxes.

 A ☐

 B ☐

 C ☐

 D ☐

 E [1]

 F ☐

 G ☐

 H ☐

1 He can ride a bike.
2 They can sing.
3 She can swim.
4 We can dance.
5 We can't dance.
6 She can't swim.
7 They can't sing.
8 He can't ride a bike.

2 ★★☆ Match the questions and answers.

0 Can you and Lucy sing? — e
1 Can you speak Spanish? — ☐
2 Can David play the piano? — ☐
3 Can Helena cook? — ☐
4 Can a Ferrari go fast? — ☐
5 Can Karim and Jake ride a bike? — ☐

a No, he can't.
b Yes, they can.
c Yes, I can.
d Yes, it can.
e No, we can't.
f Yes, she can.

3 ★★★ Write sentences with *can* or *can't*.

0 I / ride a bike (✓) / skateboard (✗)
   I can ride a bike but I can't skateboard.

1 I / sing (✓) / dance (✗)
   _____

2 my little brother / talk (✗) / walk (✓)
   _____

3 they / speak Spanish (✓) / speak French (✗)
   _____

4 my dad / drive (✗) / cook (✓)
   _____

5 we / do somersaults (✗) / spin (✓)
   _____

6 my mum / play the piano (✗) / play the guitar (✓)
   _____

7 the bird / sing (✓) / talk (✗)
   _____

Pronunciation

Long vowel sound /ɔː/
Go to page 120.

4 ★★★ Look at the pictures and write questions with *can*. Then answer them so they are true for you.

0 *Can you drive?*
Yes, I can. / No, I can't.

1 _____

2 _____

3 _____

4 _____

5 ★★★ Complete the sentences with your own ideas.

1 I can't _____ , but I can
_____ .

2 My best friend can _____ ,
but he/she can't _____ .

3 My teacher can't _____ , but
he/she can _____ .

4 Babies can _____ , but they
can't _____ .

5 My mum can _____ , but she
can't _____ .

6 My dad can't _____ , but he
can _____ .

7 The cat can _____ , but it can't
_____ .

Prepositions of time SB page 71

6 ★ ☆ ☆ (Circle) the correct options.

0 I leave home *in / on / (at)* 7 am to go to school.
1 Susie's birthday is *in / on / at* May.
2 The film starts *in / on / at* 8 pm.
3 It's very cold *in / on / at* winter.
4 I don't go to school *in / on / at* Sundays.
5 There's a holiday *in / on / at* 7ᵗʰ April this year.
6 We play tennis *in / on / at* Friday afternoons.
7 The first day of school is *in / on / at* autumn.

7 ★★ Complete the sentences with *at*, *in* or *on*.

1 The party is ____*on*____ Friday _____ 7 pm.
2 School starts _____ 8 am and it finishes _____ 3 pm.
3 It's very hot _____ summer.
4 My school holidays start _____ June and finish _____ September.
5 My birthday is _____ 21st March. It's _____ spring. This year it's _____ a Tuesday.

8 ★★ Write the words in the correct columns.

~~Friday~~ | ~~May~~ | midday | midnight | seven o'clock
September | the evening | the morning
Tuesday | ~~3.30 pm~~ | 7th July | 22nd May

in	on	at
May	Friday	3.30 pm

GET IT RIGHT! 👁

Prepositions of time

We use *on* for days of the week and dates.

✓ I go swimming **on** Saturday.
✗ I go swimming ~~in~~ Saturday.
✓ Her birthday is **on** 1st May.
✗ Her birthday is ~~in~~ 1st May.

We use *at* for clock times.

✓ My dance lesson is **at** five o'clock.
✗ My dance lesson is ~~on~~ five o'clock.

We use *in* for months and seasons.

✓ Is your birthday **in** October?
✗ Is your birthday ~~at~~ October?
✓ We often go to the beach **in** summer.
✗ We often go to the beach ~~at~~ summer.

Complete the sentences with *on*, *in* or *at*.

0 I will be there ____*on*____ Sunday evening.
1 He wants to go to your house _____ 7th July.
2 I can come _____ Monday or Friday.
3 My school exams are _____ June.
4 Can you meet me _____ half past twelve?
5 The trees are pretty _____ autumn.
6 It starts _____ quarter to ten.

VOCABULARY

Sport: ice-skate, play basketball, cycle, play volleyball, snowboard, do tae kwon do, go surfing, play rugby

Telling the time

1 It's three o'clock.

2 It's half past eight.

3 It's quarter past ten.

4 It's quarter to one.

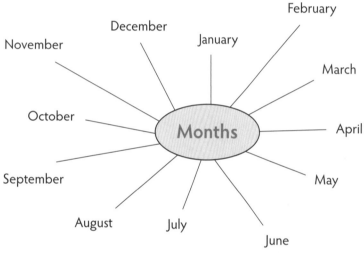

Months: December, February, January, March, April, May, June, July, August, September, October, November

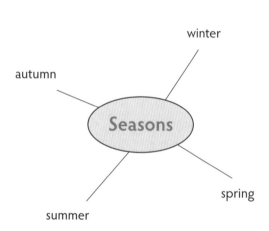

Seasons: autumn, winter, summer, spring

Ordinal numbers

1st – first	5th – fifth	9th – ninth	13th – thirteenth
2nd – second	6th – sixth	10th – tenth	20th – twentieth
3rd – third	7th – seventh	11th – eleventh	30th – thirtieth
4th – fourth	8th – eighth	12th – twelfth	31st – thirty-first

Key words in context

final	My team is in the **final**!
hit	In table tennis you **hit** a ball with a bat.
hobby	I love old photos and I collect them. It's my **hobby**.
jump	My cat can **jump** very high.
organise	Mr Thomas **organises** the Glee club at our school.
skipping rope	Lots of girls at our school like playing with **skipping ropes**.
somersault	I can't do a **somersault**. I'm not a gymnast!
spin	I like **spinning** in circles.
winner	The **winner** of the race gets $1,000.

Sport `SB page 68`

1 ★ ☆ ☆ **Look at the pictures and write sentences.**

 0 Connor
 1 Lewis
 2 Sally
 3 Adam

 4 Ethan
 5 Liz
 6 Amelia
 7 Daisy

0 *Connor ice skates.*
1 _____
2 _____
3 _____
4 _____
5 _____
6 _____
7 _____

Telling the time `SB page 69`

2 ★★ ☆ **Write the times under the clocks.**

 0
It's seven o'clock.

 1
_____

 2
_____

 3
_____

 4
_____

 5
_____

Months and seasons `SB page 71`

3 ★★ ☆ **Complete the months and seasons with the missing consonants.**

Months

1 O _ _ o _ e
2 _ u _ e
3 A _ _ i _
4 _ e _ e _ _ e
5 _ a _
6 _ u _ _
7 _ a _ u a _ _
8 A u _ u _ _
9 _ e _ _ e _ _ e _
10 _ o _ e _ _ e _
11 _ e _ _ u a _ _
12 _ a _ _ _

Seasons

13 _ u _ _ e _
14 a _ _ u _ _
15 _ _ _ i _ _
16 _ i _ _ e _

4 ★★★ **Choose four months. Say what season they are in and what you do in them in each month.**

0 *August is in summer. I go on holiday in August with my family.*

1 _____
   _____
2 _____
   _____
3 _____
   _____
4 _____
   _____

Ordinal numbers `SB page 71`

5 ★ ☆ ☆ **Complete the table.**

1st	*first*		fifth	9th			thirteen
	second	6th		10th		20th	
3rd		7th			eleventh	30th	
4th		8th		12th			thirty-first

6 ★★ ☆ **Write the ordinal numbers.**

14th *fourteenth*   21st _____   27th _____   22nd _____

28th _____   15th _____   16th _____   23rd _____

29th _____   24th _____   17th _____   18th _____

19th _____   26th _____   25th _____

READING

1 **REMEMBER AND CHECK** Match each person with two facts. Then look at the article on page 67 of the Student's Book and check your answers.

1 Nikolai Kutsenko [e]
[ ]

2 Xavier Good [ ]
[ ]

3 Tillman [ ]
[ ]

4 The Firecrackers [ ]
[ ]

a enjoys golf.
b are gymnasts.
c is a dog.
d use music for the show.
e has got a world record.
f is a little boy.
g is awesome with a football.
h can skateboard.

2 Read the text and complete the sentences under the pictures.

Sport
for All

The Paralympic Games are a big sporting event for athletes with disabilities. The games take place every two years: after the Summer Olympics, and after the Winter Olympics. They show the world all the amazing things that these athletes can do. Here are two awesome Paralympians.

This is [1]_____ .
She's from [2]_____ .

This is [3]_____ .
He's from [4]_____ .

Terezinha Guilhermina is from a poor family in Betim in Brazil. She can't see very well but she can run. She can run very fast. She runs with the help of her guide, Guilherme Soares de Santana. Guilherme can run fast, too, but he can see. He helps Terezinha keep on the track. Terezinha is very successful. She is a Paralympian gold medal winner in the 200-metre race. Now she wants to win a gold medal in her home country at the Rio 2016 Olympics.

David Weir is a wheelchair athlete from the UK. He has a problem with his legs. He can't use them to run or walk so he races in a special wheelchair. He moves the wheelchair with his hands. He races any distance from 100 metres to a full marathon. He's got six gold medals from the Paralympic Games in Beijing and London. He is also a six-time winner of the London Marathon. David is very popular with his fans. They call him the 'Weirwolf.'

3 Read the text again and answer the questions.

1 When do the Paralympics happen? _____

2 What can't Terezinha do? _____

3 Who helps Terezinha run? _____

4 What race has she got a gold medal from? _____

5 What can't David Weir do? _____

6 How does he move his wheelchair? _____

7 How many gold medals has he got from the Paralympic Games in Beijing and London? _____

DEVELOPING WRITING

An amazing person

1 **Read the text. Imagine you're the writer of the text and answer the questions.**

0 Who is he?

My cousin Tom.

1 Where is he from?

_____

2 What does he do?

_____

3 What sort of things can he do?

_____

4 Why do you like him?

_____

My cousin Tom is an amazing person. He's from Newcastle and he's the junior champion of North-East England at tae kwon do. He's only 13, but he can pick his dad up and throw him on the floor. He's got a black belt. Tom's also really good at school. He's really great at Maths and Science and he can speak three foreign languages: French, German and Spanish.

But I like Tom because he's a really good friend to me. He's also really funny and he can always make me laugh.

2 **Read the answers to the questions and use them to complete the text.**

1 Who is she?
Grandmother Ana

2 Where is she from?
Derby

3 What does she do?
swims

4 What sort of things can he/she do?
swim 400 metres in five minutes

5 Why do you like her?
friendly / makes great cakes

My ⁰ _____*Grandmother Ana*_____ is an amazing person. We live in the same town, ¹ _____ , so I see her a lot. She's 72 years old and she still ² _____ every day. She's in a team and does races most weekends. She swims in special races for people over 65. She always wins. She's really fast. She can ³ _____ .

She loves swimming. It makes her feel young.

I like her because she's really ⁴ _____ to me. And she ⁵ _____ !

3 **Answer the questions about an amazing person you know.**

1 Who is he/she?

_____

2 Where is he/she from?

_____

3 What does he/she do?

_____

4 What sort of things can he/she do?

_____

5 Why do you like him/her?

_____

4 **Use your answers to the questions in Exercise 3 to write a short text about that person. Write 35–50 words.**

_____

_____

_____

_____

_____

_____

LISTENING

1 🔊31 **Listen and match the dialogues with the pictures. Write 1–3 in the boxes.**

A ☐

B ☐

C ☐

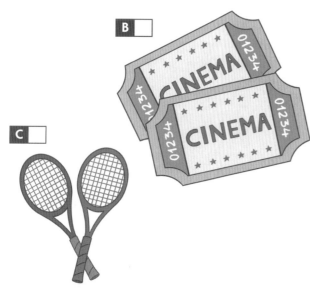

2 🔊31 **Listen again and draw the times on the clocks.**

Dialogue 1:
What time do they play tennis?

Dialogue 2:
What time is the film they choose?

Dialogue 3:
What time do they meet?

3 🔊31 **Listen again and complete each sentence with one word.**

0 Louise feels a bit ___bored___ .

1 Louise is _____ until 1 pm.

2 Tammy wants to go to the cinema in the
   _____ .

3 The first film is at _____ past six.

4 Lucy wants to go _____ with Dan.

5 Lucy finishes _____ at five.

DIALOGUE

1 **Put the dialogue in order.**

☐ BEN   We can't. I haven't got a ball.

☐ BEN   TV! That's why I'm bored. I'm tired of watching TV.

☐ BEN   We can't. She's on holiday.

1 BEN   I'm bored. What can we do?

☐ SUE   Is she? So how about some more TV?

☐ SUE   Why don't we play basketball?

☐ SUE   No ball. OK, let's go to Jenny's house.

PHRASES FOR FLUENCY SB page 73

1 **Match the questions with the answers.**

0 Are these your pens and books?   `c`

1 Oh, no, look at the rain.   ☐

2 Where's Lisbon?   ☐

3 Look, there goes the bus home. <u>Now what?</u>   ☐

a <u>It's no big deal.</u> I've got an umbrella.

b <u>I'm sure</u> it's in Portugal.

c No, I think that's Owen's <u>stuff</u>.

d Don't worry. There's another bus in 15 minutes.

2 **Complete the dialogue with the words and phrases that are underlined in Exercise 1.**

MUM   Come on, Tom. It's time for school.

TOM   I'm ready, Mum.

MUM   Have you got your swimming
      0 ___stuff___ ?

TOM   I haven't got a swimming lesson today.

MUM   1 _____ you have, Tom. It's Thursday.

TOM   Thursday! Oh, no. I have got a swimming lesson! But my towel's wet. 2 _____?

MUM   3 _____ . You can take my towel.

TOM   Thanks, Mum. You're the best.

Sum it up

1 Read and write the names of the sports.

Welcome to a day of sport on BCB TV.

We've got a great programme of sporting action for you this Saturday.

☆ We've got live   0 _football_ from Old Trafford, where Manchester United play Chelsea in the big game.

☆ We've got   1_____ – ALL the action from the NBA.

☆ There's   2_____ action from last night's match between Brazil and Spain.

☆ There's live   3_____ from one of today's Super League matches.

☆ And we've got 🛼 4_____ from Helsinki.

There's something for everyone.

2 Read the clues and complete the TV sports programme.

Start time	Finish time	Sports programme
pm	pm	
pm	pm	
pm	pm	
pm	pm	
pm	pm	

1 The afternoon of sport starts at 1 pm.
2 Rugby is the fourth programme.
3 The ice-skating is on for half an hour.
4 Football is after volleyball.
5 Basketball starts six hours after ice-skating finishes.
6 The football starts at 3 pm.
7 Rugby is two and a half hours.
8 Volleyball is an hour and a half.
9 There are eight hours of sport.
10 Ice-skating is the first sport.
11 The last programme is 90 minutes.

3 Put the words in the list into four categories. There are three words in each category. Name the categories.

~~August~~ | cycling | fifth | first | June | May | snowboarding | spring | summer | tae kwon do | third | winter

1 MONTHS	2	3	4
August			

8 DANCE TO THE MUSIC

GRAMMAR
Present continuous SB page 76

1 ★☆☆ (Circle) the correct options.

0   She isn't here. She **'s** / 're playing football in the park.

1   What *is* / *are* you doing?

2   Sorry, I can't talk now. I *'m* / *is* watching a film on TV.

3   All my friends are here. We *'s* / *'re* having a good time!

4   My brother's in his room. He *'s* / *'re* playing computer games.

5   My mum and dad *is* / *are* taking the dog for a walk.

6   I think they're happy. They *'s* / *'re* smiling a lot!

7   Look! There's Jimmy. Where *'s* / *'re* he going?

2 ★☆☆ Write the *-ing* form of these verbs.

0	shop	*shopping*	7	walk	_____
1	play	_____	8	read	_____
2	give	_____	9	take	_____
3	sit	_____	10	try	_____
4	dance	_____	11	stop	_____
5	smile	_____	12	write	_____
6	run	_____	13	draw	_____

3 ★★☆ Complete the sentences with the present continuous form of the verbs in brackets.

0   Go away Jack. I *'m not talking* to you! (not talk)

1   Let's go for a walk. It _____ . (not rain)

2   _____ you _____ the film? (enjoy)

3   _____ your brother _____ a good time at university? (have)

4   What _____ you _____, Joaquim? (do)

5   The TV is on, but they _____ it. (not watch)

6   Maria! You _____ to me! (not listen)

7   What _____ the cat _____ ? (eat)

8   They _____ well today. (not play)

4 ★★☆ Lily is telling Fred about a new quiz show on TV. Complete the dialogue with the present continuous form of the verbs in brackets.

LILY   Hey Dan, how are you? Are you free this evening?

DAN   Hmm, I'm not sure. Why?

LILY   Well, there's a great new quiz on TV. There are two teams. One player in a team ⁰ *is watching* (watch) a video on a tablet. Of course the other players can't see what ¹ _____ (happen) on the screen.

DAN   So?

LILY   Well, the player with the tablet says things like 'A boy ² _____ (run). He ³ _____ (wear) shorts. He ⁴ _____ (hold) a ball.' After each sentence the other players guess what ⁵ _____ (happen) in the video.

DAN   And then what?

LILY   The players can ask ten questions.

DAN   Like 'What ⁶ _____ they _____ (do) in the video?'

LILY   No, of course not. They can only ask questions like '⁷ _____ the boy _____ (play) with friends?' or '⁸ _____ they _____ (go) to school?' or '⁹ _____ they _____ (watch) a game of football?'

DAN   And then?

LILY   Sometimes the player watching the video says what ¹⁰ _____ (not happen) in the video. Things like 'The boy ¹¹ _____ (not sitting) on the floor' or 'The people ¹² _____ (not play) music. And the other player gets a point if they can say what's happening in the video.

DAN   Hmm. I don't like watching quiz programmes. I like watching films.

LILY   Oh. Well, please watch tonight. There's a surprise for you!

DAN   A surprise? Now I really want to watch it!

5 ★★★ Complete this extract from the quiz show with the correct form of the verbs in the list.

hit | hold | kick | not go | not smile
not throw | play (x3) | stand | ~~wear~~

HOST   Right! Let's play! Lily, you have the tablet, so your team starts.

LILY   Well, I can see twelve girls here. They 0 *'re wearing* shorts and T-shirts.

SIMON   1 _____ they _____ a game?

LILY   Yes, they are. They 2 _____ with a ball.

TOM   3 _____ they _____ the ball with their feet?

LILY   No, they aren't. And they 4 _____ the ball. One girl 5 _____ the ball in her hand. She 6 _____ behind a line on the floor.

MARK   7 _____ she _____ the ball with her hand?

LILY   Yes, she is. But the ball 8 _____ into the net. That's not good. She isn't happy. She 9 _____ .

SIMON   I know! 10 _____ they _____ volleyball?

LILY   Yes, they are!

HOST   Well done! That's one point to you.

6 ★★★ What do you think your family and friends are doing now? Look at the example and write similar sentences about them.

0 *I think my sister is watching TV now.*
1 _____
2 _____
3 _____
4 _____
5 _____

like / don't like + -ing **SB page 78**

7 ★★ Write sentences with the correct form of the verbs.

0 I / like / read / long books
   I like reading long books.
1 my sister / not like / play / basketball
   _____
2 my parents / hate / watch / science fiction films
   _____
3 my best friend / like / listen to / classical music
   _____
4 I / not like / go to / the cinema
   _____
5 I / love / read / in bed
   _____

8 ★★ Complete the text. Use *love* (☺☺), *like* (☺), *don't/doesn't like* (☹), *hate* (☹☹) and the correct form of the verbs.

My family are a bit strange – they like or don't like all kinds of different things. My sister 0 *doesn't like cooking* (☹ cook) but she 1 _____ (☺☺ clean) her room. My father 2 _____ (☹☹ go) for walks, but he 3 _____ (☺☺ go) for a ride on his bike. My mother 4 _____ (☺ read) magazines, but she 5 _____ (☹☹ read) books. My parents 6 _____ (☺ travel), but they 7 _____ (☹ go) to other countries. And me? Well, I just 8 _____ (☺☺ be) with my strange family!

9 ★★★ Complete the sentences so they are true for you.

0 I love *singing in the shower* and *going to the cinema.*
1 I love _____ and _____
2 I like _____ and _____
3 I don't like _____ and _____
4 I hate _____ and _____

GET IT RIGHT! 👁
Present continuous

We use subject + *am/is/are* + *-ing* form of the main verb.

✓ *We are watching* TV.
✗ ~~We watching TV.~~
✓ *I am eating* a sandwich.
✗ ~~I am eat a sandwich.~~

Complete the sentences with the correct present continuous form of the verbs in brackets.

0 She *is taking* (take) some photos of her cat.
1 We _____ (do) the shopping at the moment.
2 _____ (you / listen) to rap music?
3 He _____ (wear) a black shirt and trousers.
4 They _____ (walk) to the supermarket.
5 Who _____ (play) computer games?
6 He _____ (not eat) a sandwich, he's eating a burger!

VOCABULARY

Verbs

base form	-ing form
cheer	cheering
dance	dancing
leave	leaving
read	reading
run	running
sing	singing
sit	sitting
smile	smiling
stand	standing
take	taking
talk	talking
wear	wearing

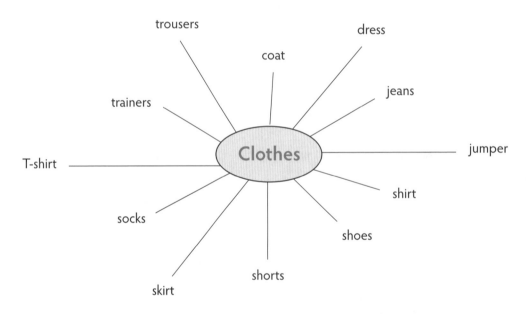

Key words in context

concert	There's a **concert** tomorrow night and it's my favourite band!
deep	The water in the swimming pool is very **deep**. It's about three metres.
hold	Please **hold** my bag, and then I can open the door.
instrument	The trumpet and the violin are musical **instruments**.
musician	He's a **musician**. He plays in a rock band.
relaxing	I love this gentle music. It's very **relaxing**.
singer	I think Taylor Swift is a very good **singer**.
size	What **size** shoes do you take?
trumpet	My brother plays the **trumpet**.
violin	She's learning to play the **violin**.

Verbs `SB page 76`

1 ★ Look at the picture above and complete the sentences with the correct form of the verbs in the list.

cheer | dance | leave | read | ~~run~~ | sing
sit | smile | stand | take | talk | wear

0   Peter is ___running___ .
1   Cindy is _____ .
2   Charles is _____ .
3   Lucy is _____ on a bench.
4   Joe and Kelly are _____ .
5   Cedric is _____ a hat.
6   Helena is _____ .
7   Rob is _____ .
8   Claire is _____ on her phone.
9   Matt is _____ a photo.
10 Fiona is _____ .
11 Jen and David are _____ the park.

2 ★★ Complete each sentence with a verb from Exercise 1. Use the correct form of the verbs.

0   I'm ___reading___ a really good magazine. It's very interesting!
1   My dad's crazy. He wants to _____ a marathon.
2   Let's _____ a song.
3   This train _____ at 10.45, and arrives in London at 12.40.
4   Look at Mike! He's _____ green trousers and a pink shirt!
5   _____ a photo of me, please.
6   I love _____ on the phone with my friends.
7   This is my favourite chair. I love _____ here.

Clothes `SB page 79`

3 ★ Find twelve clothes items in the word search.

T	R	O	U	D	E	D	J	A	N	S	T
A	S	H	I	R	T	R	A	S	E	H	P
S	A	T	H	L	O	E	W	K	S	I	O
T	R	E	A	I	N	S	X	C	R	R	R
S	N	A	E	J	O	S	H	O	E	S	E
H	T	L	O	T	S	A	U	S	S	W	P
E	R	B	K	R	H	B	N	Y	U	E	M
R	I	R	W	E	O	U	K	J	O	A	U
L	H	A	D	I	R	Y	L	U	R	F	J
P	S	C	O	A	T	T	R	N	T	E	A
J	T	R	I	K	S	G	E	S	A	R	M
U	M	B	E	T	R	A	I	N	E	R	S

4 ★★ Circle the odd one out in each list.

0   (jeans)   jumper   shirt
1   socks   trainers   coat
2   shorts   T-shirt   trousers
3   dress   skirt   shoes
4   jumper   T-shirt   coat

5 ★★ Write answers to the questions so they are true for you.

1   What colour is your favourite shirt?
    _____

2   What clothes do you love wearing at the weekend?
    _____

3   What clothes do you never buy?
    _____

4   Of all the people you know, who wears really nice clothes? What do they wear?
    _____

Pronunciation

Intonation – listing items
Go to page 120.

READING

1 REMEMBER AND CHECK **Answer the questions. Then look at the Tweets on page 75 of the Student's Book and check your answers.**

0 (09.44) What are Alex and his mum doing? _They are shopping._

1 (09.44) What is he listening to? _____

2 (09.47) A woman is sitting on a chair. What instrument is she playing?

_____

3 (09.48) Is the woman alone? _____

4 (09.49) Do the people in the supermarket like the music? _____

5 (09.53) What are people using to record the concert? _____

6 (09.53) How many girls are dancing? _____

7 (09.55) Who is leaving the supermarket? _____

2 **Read this dialogue from a TV programme. How many places does Stella visit in the studios?** _____

STELLA	Hi, everyone. Welcome to today's show. I'm at Galway Film Studios. They're making a film here and Paul Basset, the star of the film, is showing me round. Thanks a lot, Paul.
PAUL	No problem! I like showing people the place. So, first we're going to the studio where we make the films.
STELLA	There are a lot of people here. What are they all doing?
PAUL	Well, we aren't filming this afternoon. They're getting ready for tomorrow. They're cleaning and tidying the desks, and putting out the chairs. Tomorrow we're filming in an office. Those people are checking the lights.
STELLA	Where next?
PAUL	OK. This is the room for the clothes. It's called the 'wardrobe'.
STELLA	Wow! Look at all the different beautiful dresses and trousers and hats and everything. It's very tidy.
PAUL	Yes, it's difficult with so many actors. But the girls love wearing the dresses. You can see each dress has the actor's name on it. Now, we can't go in this next room, but we can look through the window. You can see the young actors.
STELLA	Yes, they're all sitting at desks, like a classroom. Are they learning their words for tomorrow?
PAUL	No, it really is a classroom. They're studying Maths and Geography.
STELLA	Why?
PAUL	Well, these kids are still at school. So they film in the mornings and have lessons in the afternoons. It's very important.
STELLA	Oh, right. Where next?
PAUL	The restaurant. I want a cup of coffee. And then we can see some more.
STELLA	Great!

3 **Read the dialogue again and mark the sentences T (true) or F (false). Correct the false statements.**

0 Stella and Paul both work in TV. [F] _Paul works in films._

1 Paul likes showing people round the studios. [ ] _____

2 Paul shows Stella the studio first. [ ] _____

3 There are actors filming in the studio. [ ] _____

4 The dresses have names on them. [ ] _____

5 The young actors in the classroom are studying for the filming tomorrow. [ ] _____

6 The young actors have lessons every afternoon. [ ] _____

7 Stella and Paul are going to the restaurant for lunch. [ ] _____

DEVELOPING WRITING

Describing a scene

1 **Read Nicole's diary entry. Who phones the writer?**

Sunday
May
30

My Sunday afternoon

It's Sunday afternoon. The sun is shining. I'm sitting in the park. I love sitting here. It's quiet and I like watching other people.

There are some children here. They're laughing and playing games. There are four people over there. They're sitting on the grass. They're having a picnic. They're having fun.

Me? I'm relaxing. It's Sunday! I've got my phone with me, and my headphones. I'm listening to music – my favourite music. In my head, I'm singing the song. I'm having a good time here. Uh, oh! Now my phone's ringing. It's my friend Steve. What does he want?

2 **Match the parts of the phrases. Then read the diary entry again and check.**

0	watching	*b*
1	playing	
2	having	
3	listening	
4	singing	

- a   a song
- b   other people
- c   games
- d   to music
- e   fun

3 **Imagine it's Sunday afternoon. Use the ideas below and make notes.**

1   Choose a place:
- the shopping centre
- the beach
- your house
- another place

2   What are you doing? What's happening near you? Who can you see and what are they doing? Use the verbs in the list to help you.

buy | have | listen | play | read | sit | watch

_____

_____

_____

_____

_____

_____

_____

3   Something happens – it changes things. What happens?

_____

_____

_____

_____

_____

_____

_____

_____

4 **Use your notes to complete the text about your Sunday afternoon.**

It's Sunday afternoon. I'm _____ .

_____ are

_____

_____

_____ .

I'm _____

_____

_____ .

Uh, oh! Now _____

_____

_____ .

LISTENING

1 🔊 33 **Listen to a boy phoning home from his holiday and answer the questions.**

1 Where is he? _____

2 Where is he going after the call?

_____

2 🔊 33 **Listen again and complete the sentences with one word.**

0 The boy's name is _Richard_ .

1 It's seven o'clock in the _____ .

2 The boys playing football are wearing _____ and _____ .

3 Two _____ are _____ bikes.

4 He thinks the men are going to

_____ .

5 The women are _____ dresses and _____ .

6 The children in the _____ are

_____ .

7 The boy is _____ to the

_____ now.

DIALOGUE

1 🔊 34 **Listen to Philip interviewing Sue for a school project. How many questions does he ask Sue?**

2 🔊 34 **Listen again and complete the dialogue.**

PHILIP   Hi, Sue! I'd like to ask you some questions.

SUE   Yeah, sure. What about?

PHILIP   What do you like doing in the evenings?

SUE   You mean, after school? Well, I like [1] _watching TV_ and I love [2] _____ .

PHILIP   And what about the weekends?

SUE   On Saturdays, I help Mum in the kitchen. I like [3] _____ , but I hate [4] _____ the dishes. And on Sundays, I like [5] _____ my friends in the shopping centre and [6] _____ to the cinema.

PHILIP   Thanks, Sue. Now I can finish my school project.

SUE   Good thing! It's only ten minutes until class!

3 **Now Philip is interviewing his granddad. Put Granddad's answers in the correct order.**

PHILIP   Granddad, can I ask you some questions, please?

GRANDDAD   Yes, of course. What do you want to know?

PHILIP   Well, what do you like doing in the evenings?

GRANDDAD   0   magazines / I / my / reading / love

I love reading my magazines.

PHILIP   And what about the weekends?

GRANDDAD   1   On / I / at / my / club / my / Saturdays / like / friends / meeting

_____

2   I / On / visit / usually / Sundays / you

_____

3   family / seeing / I / your / love

_____

4   I / don't / your music / listening / to / like / But / always

_____

PHILIP   Thanks a lot, Granddad.

4 **Imagine that Philip is interviewing you. Complete the answers to his questions so they are true for you.**

PHILIP   What do you like doing in the evenings?

YOU   I like _____ and I love

_____ .

PHILIP   What about the weekend?

YOU   On Saturday I like _____ and on Sunday I like

_____ .

PHILIP   What do you hate doing?

YOU   I hate _____ .

PHILIP   And what are you doing now?

YOU   I'm _____ .

▮▮▮ TRAIN TO THiNK ▮▮▮

Memorising

1 🔊 33   a   **Read the questions 1–5.**
   b   **Cover the questions and listen to Richard.**
   c   **Answer the questions.**
   d   **Listen to Richard again and check what you remembered.**

1 There are _____ girls playing beach volleyball.

2 There are _____ boys playing football.

3 The men on bikes are wearing _____ and

_____ .

4 There are _____ children in the sea.

5 There are _____ boys surfing.

EXAM SKILLS: Reading

Answering multiple-choice questions

1   Read Monika's email to her friend Jodie and answer the questions.

   1 Where is Monika? _____

   2 What does she want to see there? _____

Hi, Jodie

How are you? I'm on holiday – well, you know that, right? – and I'm having a great time here in Granada. We're staying in a nice hotel near the city centre. It's small but it's cheap and very comfortable, and we like it. The people who work here speak good English. That's great because my family doesn't speak Spanish! (Well, I know a few words now – *gracias* and *por favor*, that kind of thing! I can say *Tengo hambre*, too. That means 'I'm hungry', and you know me, I'm always hungry!)

Granada is a cool place. The famous Alhambra palace is here. It's very beautiful. And it's a great place for Flamenco, too. I love Flamenco dancing and I want to see some here. Oh, just a minute – my mum says that Dad is on his tablet, and he's getting tickets for a Flamenco show tonight here in the city! Great!

Hope you're well. Please write soon, OK?

From

Monika

---

2   Read the email again. Choose the correct answers (A, B or C).

   0 Monika's family are staying in a _____ hotel.
      A big   **(B)** comfortable   **C** expensive

   1 The people at the hotel _____ English.
      A like   **B** don't understand   **C** understand

   2 Monika knows _____ words in Spanish.
      A one or two   **B** a lot of   **C** no

   3 In Granada there is a famous _____ .
      A palace   **B** dance clubs   **C** cool place

   4 Monika's _____ has a tablet.
      A father   **B** mother   **C** Flamenco

   5 Monika's father _____ a Flamenco show.
      A isn't getting tickets for   **B** is buying tickets for   **C** is reading tickets for

Reading tip

When the questions about a text are multiple choice, it means you have to choose the one correct answer from three or four possibilities.

- Look for items that are grammatically wrong. For example, in the following question, A is wrong because we can't have 'a' before a vowel, and C is wrong because we can't use 'some' before a singular noun:
- He's eating _____ apple.

    A a   **B** an   **C** some

- Look for words that have similar meanings. For example, in Question 5 of Exercise 2, 'buying' and 'getting' have the same meaning.
- You must check all three or four options before you decide which the correct one is.

CONSOLIDATION

LISTENING

1 🔊 35 **Listen to Daniela and circle the correct answers (A, B or C).**

1 Daniela's birthday is …
   A 20th October.
   B 21st October.
   C 1st October.

2 Daniela's camera is a present from …
   A her grandparents.
   B her brother.
   C her mother and father.

3 Daniela's favourite season is …
   A winter.
   B autumn.
   C summer.

2 🔊 35 **Listen again and complete the words.**

1 Daniela is f_____ .

2 She thinks Ipswich isn't e_____ .

3 Daniela is having d_____ lessons.

4 Daniela's got special s_____ for dancing.

5 Daniela's friends like s_____ .

6 Daniela likes w_____ on cold days.

GRAMMAR

3 **Circle the correct options.**

SUE   Hi, Alex. What [1]*are / is* you doing?

ALEX Oh, hi, Sue. [2]*I wait / I'm waiting* for my bus. And you?

SUE   I'm doing some shopping. I'm not [3]*buying / buy* much – just some food. Hey, you've got headphones. Cool!

ALEX Oh, yeah. [4]*I'm listening / I listen* to some music. I mean, waiting for the bus is boring! I [5]*can't / don't can* wait without music!

SUE   What [6]*do you listen / are you listening* to right now?

ALEX It's some piano music. I really like [7]*listen / listening* to piano music.

SUE   [8]*Can you / Do you can* play the piano, Alex?

ALEX No, I [9]*can't / can*. But I always [10]*listen / am listening* to it!

4 ★★ **Fred is showing Lily a video on his phone. Put the words in order to make sentences.**

0 is / Alice / sister / This / my
   This is my sister Alice.

1 driving / She / her car / is
   _____

2 is / an old people's home / She / going to
   _____

3 is / at the old people's home / She / giving / a concert
   _____

4 She's / some / the guitar / of her friends / playing / with
   _____

5 a chair / is / on / Alice / sitting
   _____

6 next to / is / her / My brother Pete / standing
   _____

7 Beatles / singing / songs / They're / old
   _____

8 are / The / with / them / old people / singing
   _____

VOCABULARY

5 **Put the words in the list into three groups. Give each group a title. Then write one more word in each group.**

August | dress | February | golf | gymnastics | jeans
jumper | June | May | surfing | tennis | trainers

1 *months*	2	3

6 **Complete the sentences with the words in the list. There are two extra words.**

cheer | dance | dancing | second | summer
talk | two | watching

1 My birthday is the _____ of September.

2 I've got a problem with my leg, so I can't _____ tonight.

3 Every day, I _____ to my grandfather for ten minutes on the phone.

4 I like listening to music but I don't like _____ to it.

5 We always _____ when our team wins a game.

6 It's great here in the _____ when the weather is hot.

DIALOGUE

7 Put the dialogues in order.

Dialogue 1

☐	TANYA	No, I don't like watching TV. It's all sport and stuff.
☐	TANYA	No, it's seven o'clock. The shops close at half past seven.
1	TANYA	I'm really bored.
☐	GRAHAM	Me too. Why don't we go into town? We can go shopping.
☐	GRAHAM	That's right. OK, let's watch TV then.

Dialogue 2

☐	STEVE	OK, it's no big deal. We can stay here in the house. I've got a good book to read.
☐	STEVE	Hey, how about going for a walk?
☐	STEVE	Yes, I'm sure I can find one for you.
☐	DORA	Good idea. I like reading. Have you got a book for me, too?
☐	DORA	No thanks! It's cold outside. And I don't like walking very much.

READING

8 Read the phone dialogue. Then complete the sentences with the correct information.

ROGER	Hey Monica, what are you doing?
MONICA	I'm talking to you on the phone, ha, ha!
ROGER	Yes, very funny. But seriously – what are you doing?
MONICA	Nothing really. I'm just sitting in my room. Why?
ROGER	How about coming to the park? That's where I am now!
MONICA	The park? Why? What's happening in the park?
ROGER	There's a race today. It's a ten-kilometre run. My parents are running in it.
MONICA	Are they crazy? It's winter! It's cold and it's raining.
ROGER	It isn't raining very much. And I'm wearing a warm coat and shoes. So I'm OK.
MONICA	Well, no thanks. I like being warm, not cold.
ROGER	OK, it's no big deal. Oh, I can see Mark Watson. He's running in the race, too.
MONICA	Really? Mark Watson from our school?
ROGER	Yes, him. And he's first – he's winning!
MONICA	OK, I'm putting my coat on and I'm leaving the house now.
ROGER	Really?
MONICA	Yes – Mark Watson's there, so I want to be there, too!
ROGER	Oh, OK. See you soon then!

1 Monica is in _____ .

2 Roger is in _____ .

3 There's a _____ -kilometre race today.

4 Roger's _____ and _____ are running in the race.

5 Roger _____ cold because he's _____ a warm coat.

6 Monica doesn't like _____ .

7 Mark Watson is a boy from their _____ .

8 Mark is _____ the race.

9 Monica is _____ the house because she wants to _____ .

WRITING

9 **Write a short dialogue between two friends. Use these ideas to help you.**
- one friend is bored
- the other friend suggests something to do
- the first friend doesn't like the idea very much
- the second friend suggests another thing to do (go for a walk, go to the cinema, play video games, etc.)

9 | WOULD YOU LIKE DESSERT?

GRAMMAR

must / mustn't SB page 86

1 ★☆☆ **Complete the sentences with *must* or *mustn't*.**

My very healthy mum says:

0 I _mustn't_ drink too much cola.

1 I _____ eat more salad.

2 I _____ eat chocolate or sweets before meals.

3 I _____ go to bed late.

4 I _____ do sports after school.

5 I _____ drink more water.

2 ★★☆ **Circle the correct options.**

0 A Mum, have we got any fruit?

   B No, we haven't. I **must** / mustn't buy some.

1 A Do you want to come to my house after school?

   B I can't. I've got a piano lesson tomorrow so I *must* / *mustn't* practise tonight.

2 A What day is it today?

   B It's Thursday. We've got football this afternoon. You *must* / *mustn't* forget your football boots.

3 A What a cute dog! Can we take it home?

   B OK, but it *must* / *mustn't* stay outside.

4 A I'm not ready yet.

   B Hurry up then. We *must* / *mustn't* miss the bus.

5 A I'm ready, Mum.

   B Good. The play starts in half an hour and we *must* / *mustn't* be late.

6 A Hey Dad, can I have one of these apples?

   B Yes, but you *must* / *mustn't* wash your hands before you eat it.

3 ★★★ **Complete the sentences with *must* (✓) or *mustn't* (✗) and a verb from the list.**

be | buy | eat | finish | forget | give
remember | wash | ~~write~~

0 Ellie _must write_ an email to her friend Jasmine in Istanbul. (✓)

1 Marcus _____ late home today. (✗)

2 Helen _____ to take her tablet to school. (✓)

3 Oscar and Ellie _____ to tidy their bedrooms. (✗)

4 Marcus _____ the book back to James. (✓)

5 Hermione and Ellie _____ a present for their friend Jane. (✓)

6 Oscar _____ his homework before dinner. (✓)

7 We _____ any food in the classroom. (✗)

8 We _____ our hands before we eat lunch. (✓)

4 ★★★ **Write five things you *must* or *mustn't* do this year.**

0 *I must learn some new English words.* _____

1 _____

2 _____

3 _____

4 _____

5 _____

can (asking for permission) SB page 87

5 ★☆☆ **Put the words in order to make questions.**

0 we / Can / the football match / Saturday / on / go / to
   Can we go to the football match on Saturday?

1 have / I / Can / an egg / breakfast / for
   _____

2 we / Can / invite / Tom / to / my birthday party
   _____

3 go / we / Can / the cinema / to / school / after
   _____

4 phone / I / Can / my mum
   _____

5 I / wear / Can / blue / jumper / your / tomorrow
   _____

6 ★★ Match the children's questions with Dad's answers. Draw lines.

0 Can I take your laptop to school with me?

1 Can we go swimming on Saturday?

2 Can I go to Karen's after school tonight?

3 Can Mike and I go climbing this weekend?

a No, we can't. The pool is closed this weekend.

b Yes, of course you can. But don't come home late.

c Well, OK. But be careful.

d No, you can't. I need it for work.

I'd like … / Would you like …? SB page 89

7 ★ Write sentences using would/'d like.

0 I / vegetable soup
I'd like vegetable soup.

1 my mum / steak and chips
_____

2 what / you / for dessert / ?
_____

3 Dad / ice cream for dessert / ?
_____

8 ★★ Put the dialogue in order.

☐ WAITER *(five minutes later)* Are you ready to order?

☐ WAITER Four soups, OK. And what would you like for the main course?

☐ WAITER And finally, any drinks?

☐ WAITER OK, so would you like a starter?

1 WAITER Good evening. Would you like a table for four?

☐ CUSTOMER Yes, please.

☐ CUSTOMER Yes, we are.

☐ CUSTOMER Just water for everyone.

☐ CUSTOMER We'd like one chicken salad, one steak and chips, one pizza and one burger with potatoes and vegetables, please.

☐ CUSTOMER Yes, please. We'd like two tomato soups and two vegetable soups.

Pronunciation

Intonation – giving two choices

Go to page 121.

9 ★★★ Look at the menu on page 88 of the Student's Book and complete the dialogue so it is true for you.

WAITER Are you ready to order?

YOU Yes, I am.

WAITER Would you like a starter?

YOU Yes, please. _____

WAITER And what would you like for the main course?

YOU _____

WAITER And would you like a dessert?

YOU Yes, please. _____

WAITER Any drinks?

YOU Yes, _____ .

GET IT RIGHT! ◉
like and would like

We use *like* to say that something is nice.
✓ I *like* ice cream. It's yummy!

We use *would like* to ask for something we want or to ask somebody what they want.
✓ I *would like* an ice cream, please.
✗ ~~I like~~ an ice cream, please.
✓ *Would* you *like* an ice cream?
✗ ~~You like~~ an ice cream?

Circle the correct options.

0 I *like* / *would like* to come to your house tomorrow.

1 I *like* / *would like* a dog for my birthday.

2 I *like* / *would like* this house and I'm happy living here.

3 I *like* / *would like* travelling to different countries.

4 I *like* / *would like* to go shopping on Monday.

5 I'm thirsty. I *like* / *would like* a drink of water.

6 When I have time, I *like* / *would like* reading.

VOCABULARY

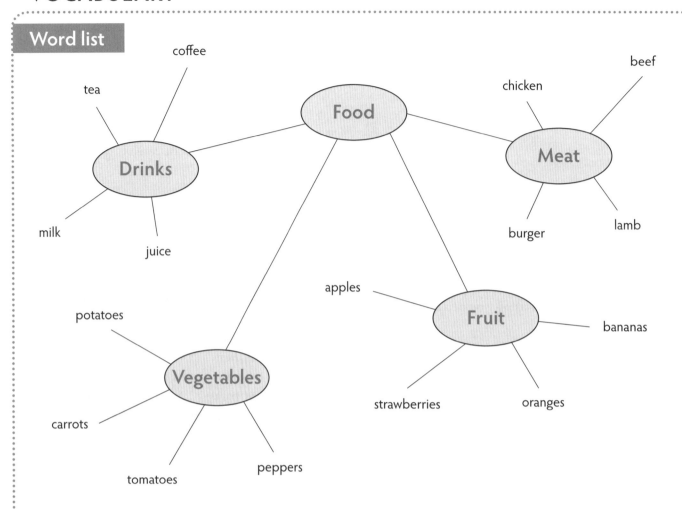

coffee

tea

Food

chicken

beef

Drinks

Meat

milk

juice

burger

lamb

apples

Fruit

bananas

potatoes

Vegetables

strawberries

oranges

carrots

tomatoes

peppers

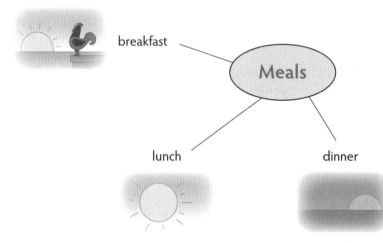

breakfast

Meals

lunch

dinner

Key words in context

a bit of	There is only **a bit of** cheese on the jacket potato.
be careful	**Be careful.** Don't spill the tea.
borrow	Can I **borrow** your laptop?
butter	I like **butter** and jam on my toast.
cereal	I usually have **cereal** with milk for breakfast.
dessert	I'd like chocolate ice cream for **dessert**.
honey	I often have bread and **honey** for breakfast.
menu	Great. There's pizza on the **menu** today.
order	Are you ready to **order**?
starter	Would you like a **starter**?

Food and drink `SB page 86`

1 ★ Look at the pictures and complete the puzzle. What's the mystery sentence?

The mystery sentence is:

_____

2 ★★ Unscramble the words and complete the sentences.

0 It's ___*beef*___ with potatoes and vegetables for lunch today. (e b e f)

1 My mum doesn't like _____ . (b l a m)

2 I often drink _____ for breakfast. (l i m k)

3 I sometimes have an _____ after dinner. (p l p a e)

4 I'd like _____ and ice cream for dessert. (s t a r w b i r r e e s)

5 I like vegetables but I don't like _____ . (a c o r r t s)

Meals `SB page 89`

3 ★ Find and (circle) nine breakfast items in the word snake.

4 ★★ Put the words in order to make sentences.

0 you / do / usually / eat / for / breakfast, / What / Debbie / ?
What do you usually eat for breakfast, Debbie?

1 always / I / eat / an / egg / breakfast / for

2 usually / I / eat / toast

3 you / lunch / usually / have / for / What / do / ?

4 often / I / have / jacket potato / a

5 sometimes / have / I / steak / chips / vegetables / and / with

6 do / you / What / usually / drink / meals, / with / your / Debbie / ?

7 drink / I / usually / or water / fruit juice

8 never / I / drink / coffee

5 ★★ Tick (✓) the things Debbie has for breakfast and lunch in Exercise 4.

☐ fruit   ☐ toast   ☐ an egg
☐ water   ☐ coffee   ☐ pizza
☐ spaghetti   ☐ vegetables   ☐ jacket potato
☐ fruit juice ☐ yoghurt   ☐ cereal
☐ steak   ☐ chicken   ☐ chips

6 ★★★ Write sentences about Greg and Jamie using the words in brackets.

	always	often	sometimes	never
breakfast	an egg	toast	cereal	yoghurt
lunch	coffee	a sandwich	pizza	soup
dinner	soup	pasta	fish and chips	salad

0 They *sometimes have cereal for breakfast.* (sometimes)

1 _____ (always)

2 _____ (often)

3 _____ (never)

4 _____ (sometimes)

5 _____ (often)

READING

1 `REMEMBER AND CHECK` **Answer the questions. Then look at the article on page 85 of the Student's Book and check your answers.**

0 What's the name of the TV programme?
 Star Junior Chefs

1 How old is Harry?
 _____

2 Where is he from?
 _____

3 How old must you be to go on the show?
 _____

4 What does Harry cook this time?
 _____

5 What time does the show finish?
 _____

2 **Read the leaflet for Cooking camp. What can you learn to make? Tick (✓) the correct photos.**

MID-TERM HOLIDAY COOKING CAMP

28th, 29th & 30th October

Mornings (3 days) 10 am–1 pm (ages 11–14 years) £45 per week

Learn to make CAKES, BREAD, PIZZA, PASTA, HEALTHY SOUPS & FRUIT SMOOTHIES
Marianne is an excellent cook and she loves good food. She has got family from Spain, Turkey, Italy and Russia. She loves food from all those countries. Come and learn to cook with her.
You must be 11–14 years old.

You must love food.
You must wear a chef's hat.
You mustn't be late. There's a lot to learn.
And remember! Cooking is fun!

Call 0123 6564 to book a place.

3 **Read the leaflet again. Then correct the sentences.**

0 Cooking camp is in November.
 Cooking camp is in October.

1 Cooking camp is for three afternoons.
 _____

2 You don't make any drinks.
 _____

3 Marianne has got family from Germany.
 _____

4 You must be 8–11 years old.
 _____

5 You mustn't wear any special clothes.
 _____

6 You mustn't be on time.
 _____

7 Remember that cooking is important.
 _____

4 **Complete the questionnaire for the Cooking camp so it is true for you.**

COOKING CAMP QUESTIONNAIRE

1 What's your name? _____

2 How old are you? _____

3 What is your favourite dish? _____

4 Do you help your parents in the kitchen?
 _____

5 Can you cook? _____

6 What can you cook? _____
 _____

DEVELOPING WRITING

My meal plan

1 **Plan three meals for the day. Write your food choices in the columns. Use the words in the list and your own ideas.**

bread | burger | cereal | chicken | chips
chocolate | chocolate cake | coffee | cola
eggs | fish | fruit | fruit juice | honey | ice cream
jacket potato | jam | pizza | salad | tea | toast
vegetables | vegetable soup | yoghurt

Breakfast	Lunch	Dinner

2 **Read the text about Sam's lunch. Then answer the questions.**

I often eat a healthy lunch. I never eat burgers and chips. Sometimes I eat fish and sometimes I eat chicken. I always eat salad or vegetables with my meal. For dessert, I usually have fruit. Today it's an apple. But sometimes I have ice cream. My favourite is strawberry ice cream. I always have a drink with my meal. I usually drink water but I sometimes have orange juice. I never drink cola.

0 How often does Sam eat burger and chips?
He never eats burgers and chips.

1 What fruit has he got for lunch today?

_____

2 What is his favourite ice cream?

_____

3 What does he always have with his meal?

_____

4 What does he usually drink with his meal?

_____

3 **Complete the diagram with the words from Exercise 1.**

not very healthy
burgers

juice

very healthy
oranges

4 **Use your notes in Exercise 3 to complete a healthy meal plan.**

Every day, I eat a healthy _____ .
Sometimes I eat _____ and
sometimes I eat _____ . I always
eat _____ with my meal. I don't
like _____ or _____ .
For dessert, I usually have _____ .
But sometimes I have _____ .
I really like _____ . I usually
have a drink with my meal. I usually
drink _____ but I sometimes
have _____ . I never drink
_____ .

Writing tip

Add more detail to your writing by using adverbs of frequency.

● How often do you eat things?
You can answer this question with *always, usually, sometimes* and *never*.
I **sometimes** have fish for lunch.
I **never** drink cola.
I **usually** have fruit for dessert.
I **always** have vegetables with my meal.

LISTENING

1 🔊**37** Listen and ⟨circle⟩ the correct options to complete the menu.

RIVER PARK CAFÉ

- Menu -

STARTERS
[1]*Tomato / Carrot* Soup
Vegetable Soup

MAIN COURSE
Steak & [2]*Chips / Vegetables*
Jacket potato with [3]*chicken / cheese*
[4]*Beef / Chicken* salad
Fish & chips
[5]*Pizza / Pasta* with tomato sauce
Omelette with peppers

DESSERT
[6]*Chocolate / Carrot* cake
[7]*Strawberries / Bananas* & ice cream

DRINKS
[8]*Lemon / Apple* juice
Orange juice
Pot of [9]*tea / coffee* for one
Water

2 🔊**37** Listen again. Mark the sentences T (true) or F (false).

0	The girl orders chocolate cake for dessert.	F
1	The boy doesn't like tomatoes.	
2	He likes eggs so he orders the omelette.	
3	He orders strawberries with ice cream for dessert.	
4	She orders a pot of coffee.	
5	He orders apple juice.	

DIALOGUE

1 ⟨Circle⟩ the correct options.

WAITER	Are you ready to [1]*sit down / order*?
CUSTOMER 1	Yes, we are.
WAITER	Would you like a [2]*starter / main course*?
CUSTOMER 1	Yes, please. I'd like tomato soup.
CUSTOMER 2	And I'd like vegetable soup.
WAITER	And what would you like for the [3]*dessert / main course*?
CUSTOMER 1	I'd like chicken salad, please.
CUSTOMER 2	And I'd like fish and chips, please.
WAITER	And for [4]*starter / dessert*?
CUSTOMER 1	We'd like chocolate cake, please.
WAITER	Any [5]*drinks / desserts*?
CUSTOMER 1	Yes, please. I'd like apple juice.
CUSTOMER 2	And I'd like water.

PHRASES FOR FLUENCY

SB page 91

1 Complete the dialogues with the phrases in the list.

Of course. | Be careful! | a bit of | the thing is

Dialogue 1
A Can you take these plates to the table?
B OK.
A _____ Don't drop them.
B Yes, Dad.

Dialogue 2
A What's for dinner?
B It's pizza.
A Oh, no.
B What's wrong with pizza? I love it.
A Well, _____ , I don't like tomatoes.

Dialogue 3
A Is there any cheese on the jacket potato?
B Yes, there is and there's _____ butter, too.

Dialogue 4
A Would you like some vegetables with your steak?
B _____ I love vegetables.

Sum it up

1 Unscramble the letters to find the food.

What's on Paul's pizza?

0 s e e c h e — *cheese*

1 r e p s p e p — ____

2 k i c e n c h — ____

3 o e s t o m t a — ____

What would Sally like for dinner?

4 k e a s t — ____

5 t o p o e s t a — ____

6 d a s a l — ____

What's in David's dessert?

7 c o c h l a t e o — ____

8 c i e r e c a m — ____

9 r a w s t e r r i e b s — ____

10 n a b a n a — ____

CAFÉ

____

STARTERS

____

____

MAIN COURSES

____

____

____

DRINKS

____

____

____

DESSERTS

____

____

____

2 Write a menu. Use food and drink words from the unit.

- Think of a name for your café.
- Create a milkshake or a smoothie.
- Make a special pizza for your café.
- Create meals with the food words.
- Create one unusual meal.

For example: *Strawberry and Orange Salad or Carrot and Orange Soup*

3 Imagine you have a customer at your café. Complete the dialogue.

WAITER — Hello and welcome to _____ Café.

CUSTOMER 1 — Hello. We'd like a table for two.

WAITER — OK. Follow me, please.

(5 minutes later)

WAITER — Are you ready to order now?

CUSTOMER 1 — Yes, we are.

WAITER — Would you like a starter?

CUSTOMER 1 — Yes, please. _____ and my friend _____ .

WAITER — And what _____ for the main course?

CUSTOMER 1 — _____ , please.

CUSTOMER 2 — And _____ .

WAITER — And for dessert?

CUSTOMER 1 — _____ , please.

CUSTOMER 2 — And _____ .

WAITER — Any drinks?

CUSTOMER 1 — Yes, please. _____ and my friend _____ .

10 HIGH FLYERS

GRAMMAR

Past simple: *was / wasn't; were / weren't; there was / were* `SB page 94`

1 ★☆☆ (Circle) the correct options.

0 You *was / (were)* late.
1 It *wasn't / weren't* his dog.
2 I *was / were* at home yesterday.
3 We *was / were* at a football match.
4 They *wasn't / weren't* at the cinema last night.
5 She *was / were* my best friend.

2 ★★☆ Complete the sentences with *was, were, wasn't* or *weren't*.

0 I _____was_____ (✓) born in Paris.
1 My grandma _____ (✗) an astronaut.
2 Andy and Jay _____ (✓) in the park yesterday.
3 We _____ (✗) at my aunt's house last night.
4 Leon _____ (✗) at the football match on Sunday.
5 It _____ (✓) my birthday yesterday.

3 ★★★ Complete the text with *was(n't)* or *were(n't)*.

The Montgolfier brothers ⁰_____were_____ the inventors of the hot-air balloon. They ¹_____ (✓) French. Their names ²_____ (✓) Joseph-Michel and Jacques-Étienne. Joseph-Michel ³_____ (✓) born in 1740, and Jacques-Étienne ⁴_____ (✓) born in 1745. There ⁵_____ (✓) sixteen children in the family. Their father ⁶_____ (✗) an inventor. He ⁷_____ (✓) a paper manufacturer.

The first balloon flight ⁸_____ (✓) in June 1783. There ⁹_____ (✗) any passengers. There ¹⁰_____ (✓) no one on the balloon. The second flight ¹¹_____ (✓) in Paris in September 1783. This time, there ¹²_____ (✓) three passengers, but the passengers ¹³_____ (✗) people. They ¹⁴_____ (✓) a chicken, a duck and a sheep.

Past simple: *Was he …? / Were you …?* `SB page 95`

4 ★☆☆ Match the questions with the answers.

0	Were you born in London?	e
1	Was your grandfather a chef?	
2	Was Valentina an astronaut?	
3	Was it your dog?	
4	Was I late to the party?	
5	Were you and I on time?	
6	Were Sam and Joe at the club yesterday?	

a No, he wasn't.
b Yes, you were!
c Yes, it was.
d No, we weren't.
e Yes, I was.
f No, they weren't.
g Yes, she was.

5 ★★☆ Put the words in order to make questions. Then look at the text in Exercise 3 and answer the questions.

0 Were / the / inventors / brothers / Montgolfier
   Were the Montgolfier brothers inventors?
   Yes, they were.

1 they / Italian / Were
   _____
   _____

2 Was / Joseph-Michel / in 1740 / born
   _____
   _____

3 Was / inventor / an / their / father
   _____
   _____

4 the / Was / in / flight / first / June 1795
   _____
   _____

5 flight / second / Prague / in / Was / the
   _____
   _____

6 Were / there / passengers / any
   _____
   _____

Past simple: regular verbs SB page 97

6 ★ Complete the table with the past simple of the verbs in the list.

believe | carry | cry | finish | help
like | live | study | ~~work~~

+ -ed	+ -d	+ -ied
worked		

7 ★★ Put the words in order to make sentences. Put the verbs in the past simple.

0 uncle / My / study / university / at / medicine
My uncle studied medicine at university.

1 finish / degree / his / He / 2010 / in

2 at / hospital / a / He / work / Birmingham / in

3 in / He / Madrid / three / years / for / live

4 like / He / Spain / very / much

5 move / He / London / to / 2014 / in

8 ★★ Complete the sentences with the past simple form of the verbs in brackets.

Name: Weather Girl
Profession: Superhero TV Presenter
Powers: She can change the weather.

Weather Girl [0] ___*lived*___ (live) in London. She [1]_____ (study) Geography at university. She [2]_____ (work) for the BBC. One night, she [3]_____ (walk) home in the rain. Suddenly, a car [4]_____ (crash) into a wall. Weather Girl [5]_____ (phone) for an ambulance. They [6]_____ (wait) for the ambulance in the rain. It was wet and cold. `Please stop the rain,' she [7]_____ (cry). Suddenly, the clouds [8]_____ (move) away, and there was no more rain. That night, Weather Girl [9]_____ (discover) her super powers.

Pronunciation

Past simple regular verbs
Go to page 121.

9 ★★ Complete the text with the past simple form of the verbs in brackets.

Florence Nightingale

Florence Nightingale [0] ___*was*___ (be) a famous English nurse. She [1]_____ (be) born in Florence in Italy in 1820. Later, her parents [2]_____ (move) back to England. As a child, she [3]_____ (like) helping others. She [4]_____ (care) for sick people and animals. She [5]_____ (want) to be a nurse.
In 1851, she [6]_____ (work) as a nurse in Germany. In 1853, there [7]_____ (be) a war. It [8]_____ (be) called the Crimean War. They [9]_____ (need) nurses, so Florence [10]_____ (sail) with nurses to help. They [11]_____ (look) after the British soldiers there. Life [12]_____ (not be) easy. The war [13]_____ (end) in 1856. Florence Nightingale [14]_____ (return) to England as a hero. She [15]_____ (die) in London in 1910.

GET IT RIGHT!

was/wasn't and **were/weren't**

We use *was*, *wasn't*, *were* and *weren't* to talk about the past. We use *am*, *am not*, *is*, *isn't*, *are* and *aren't* to talk about now.

✓ Yesterday **was** my birthday.
✗ Yesterday *is* my birthday.

Correct the sentences.

0 Jeff isn't at school yesterday.
    Jeff wasn't at school yesterday.

1 There is a great film on TV last night.

2 Hello! I was very happy to see you.

3 All my friends are there for my birthday last night.

4 Is Ian with you yesterday evening?

5 Jenny was worried about her exam today.

6 They aren't late for school yesterday.

VOCABULARY

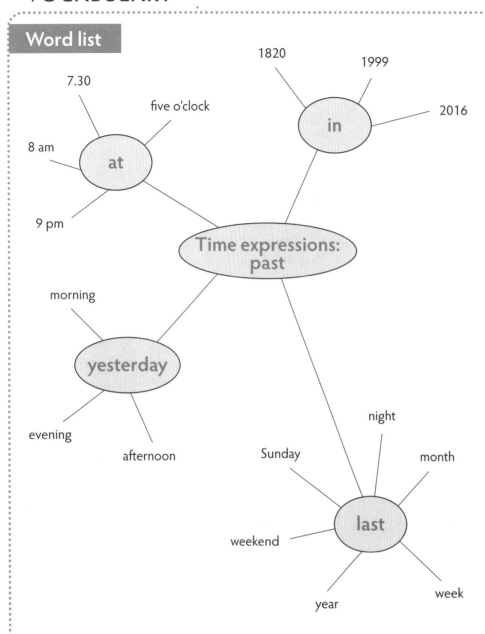

Time expressions: past

- at — 7.30, five o'clock, 8 am, 9 pm
- in — 1820, 1999, 2016
- yesterday — morning, evening, afternoon
- last — Sunday, night, month, weekend, year, week

The weather

It's sunny.

It's hot.

It's snowing.

It's cold.

It's cloudy.

It's raining.

It's windy.

It's warm.

Key words in context

arrive	We **arrived** home at six o'clock.
astronaut	I'd love to be an **astronaut** and fly to the moon.
born	I was **born** in 2002. My birthday is on the 22nd June.
call	We've got a dog and we **call** it Henry.
decide	James **decided** to work hard at school.
die	Walt Disney **died** in 1966.
flight	We are going to Madrid by plane. The **flight** is three hours.
monster	The **monster** in the story has got one eye.
space	You need a special plane to travel in **space**.
storm	There was a big **storm** last night.
strange	First it was sunny, then it rained, then it snowed. It was a **strange** day.
work	Annie **worked** in a hospital. She was a doctor.

Time expressions: past SB page 94

1 ★ Complete the table with the words in the list.

afternoon | evening | ~~month~~ | morning
night | Saturday | three o'clock | year
6 pm | 10.30 | 1969 | 2015

last	in
month	
at	**yesterday**

2 ★ Complete the dialogues with *in*, *at*, *yesterday* and *last*.

0

A Where were you _____*last*_____ night?

B I was at home.

1

A Were you at school _____
afternoon?

B Yes, I was.

2

A Was James at the party _____
Saturday?

B No, he was at home.

3

A Was your dad born _____ 1980?

B No, he wasn't.

4

A Was Tim still at school _____ 5 pm
this evening?

B Yes, he was.

3 ★★ Where were you? Write sentences with *at*, *last* and *yesterday* and the time if necessary.

0 (at) *I was on the bus at eight o'clock.*

1 (at) _____

2 (last) _____

3 (yesterday) _____

The weather SB page 97

4 ★★ Complete the crossword.

ACROSS

4 Today it's _____, so no need for sunglasses.

5 It's _____, so don't forget your umbrella.

7 It's _____, so it's a great day to fly your kite.

8 It's _____ – there are lots of people on the beach today.

DOWN

1 Today is lovely and _____. Let's sit outside.

2 Drink lots of water today – It's very _____!

3 You can make a snowman today. It's _____.

4 It's _____ today, so don't forget to wear warm clothes.

5 ★★ Circle the correct options in these phone dialogues.

1

A What's the weather like?

B It's [0]*sunny* / *cloudy*. I'm wearing sunglasses.

A Is it [1]*cold* / *hot*?

B Yes, it is. I'm wearing a T-shirt. What's the weather like there?

A It's very [2]*cloudy* / *windy* here. Listen. Can you hear it?

B Yes, I can.

2

A What's the weather like?

B It's [3]*raining* / *cloudy*. I can't walk the dog outside today.

A Is it [4]*cold* / *hot*?

B Yes, it is. I'm wearing a jumper and a coat. What's the weather like there?

A It's [5]*snowing* / *windy* here. We can't go to school today because we can't get out of the house.

B Really?

6 ★★★ Write a sentence about the weather today.

_____

_____

READING

1 **REMEMBER AND CHECK** Answer the questions. Then look at the article on page 93 of the Student's Book and check your answers.

0 Where was Valentina Tereshkova born? *She was born in Russia.*

1 What was her mother's job? _____

2 What was Valentina's job? _____

3 What was her hobby? _____

4 When was her first flight in space? _____

5 How many days was she in space? _____

6 What was her face on? _____

7 When did she carry the Olympic flag? _____

2 Read the article about the superhero *Weather Girl*. Find and write the words.

1 a season: _____

2 three weather words: _____ _____ _____

Weather Girl

Her real name is Milly Moon but people call her Weather Girl. They call her Weather Girl because she can control the weather. (**A**) She can control the clouds and the wind. When Weather Girl uses her powers, she saves people's lives. She's a superhero.

Milly Moon was born on the 31st December, 1995. It was winter and it was a cold and windy day. That night, there was a big snow storm. Mr and Mrs Moon walked home with their new baby girl. (**B**) But baby Milly wasn't cold. She was warm. Her parents were surprised. 'She's a very special baby', they decided. And they were right.

Milly Moon lived with her parents and her sister in a small town in Canada. When she was 16, she used her special powers for the first time. One day, there was a lot of snow. It was her sister Jojo's birthday. Jojo was very sad. She wanted a party but there was too much snow. Milly Moon looked out of the window at the snow. She closed her eyes and counted to ten. Then she opened them. (**C**) 'Look Jojo! You can have your party now.' Jojo was happy again.

Milly was always interested in the weather. She studied Geography at university. (**D**) She studied the weather day and night. One night, there was a lot of rain, so much that it filled people's houses. (**E**) Now, Milly often uses her special powers and she helps a lot of people.

3 Read the article again. Match the sentences with the correct places (A–E).

0 Suddenly, there wasn't any snow. [C]

1 Then she worked at a local TV station as a weather girl. [ ]

2 She can make rain or snow. [ ]

3 They were very cold and they nearly died. [ ]

4 Weather Girl stopped the rain and she saved four people's lives. [ ]

DEVELOPING WRITING

A short biography

1 Use the information in the list to complete the factfile.

actor | American | ~~Christopher Reeve~~
four Superman films | New York City
the superhero, Superman |
25th September 1952 | 52
1978 | 1987 | 2004

Superman

Name: *Christopher Reeve*

Nationality:

Place of birth:

Date of birth:

Job:

Played:

Acted in:

Date of his first Superman film:

Date of his last Superman film:

Died:

Age:

2 Look at Exercise 1 and complete the short biography of Christopher Reeve.

His name was _____ . He
was _____ . He was born in
_____ on _____ . He was an
_____ . He played _____ .
He acted in _____ . His first
Superman film was in _____ and
his last film was in _____ . He died
in _____ . He was _____
years old.

3 Look at the notes about Spider-Man and Tobey Maguire. Then use the notes to write a short biography of him.

Spider-Man

Name: Tobey Maguire

Nationality: American

Place of birth: California

Date of birth: 27th June 1975

Job: actor

Played: the superhero, Spider-Man

Acted in: three Spider-Man films

First Spider-Man film: 2002

Last Spider-Man film: 2007

LISTENING

1 Look at the picture and guess the answers to the questions.

1 Who is the man in the photo? _____

2 What did he write about? _____

2 🔊39 Listen to Tom talking about his hero. Circle the the correct options.

0 Tom's hero was a (writer) / artist.

1 His most famous book was *Narnia* / *The Jungle Book*.

2 His parents were *English* / *Indian*.

3 His father was *a doctor* / *an artist*.

4 Rudyard Kipling *loved* / *hated* India.

5 He was *happy* / *unhappy* with the Holloways.

6 He *loved* / *hated* books.

7 He was *happy* / *unhappy* at school in Devon.

8 After school he lived in *Italy* / *India*.

9 He worked for a *newspaper* / *university*.

3 🔊39 Listen again and complete the text with the correct words.

> Rudyard Kipling's parents were English. They ⁰ _*moved*_ to India. His father was an artist and he worked at a School of Art in Mumbai. Kipling loved India. He loved the ¹_____ and the culture. However, he didn't have a happy childhood. His parents wanted him to go to ²_____ in England. When he was six years old, he lived with a ³_____ , the Holloways in a seaside ⁴_____ in England. Mrs Holloway was very bad to him. He ⁵_____ life there and he was very unhappy. Luckily he ⁶_____ books. He loved books. They ⁷_____ him from his unhappy life.

DIALOGUE

1 Complete the dialogue with the past simple of the verbs in brackets. Then put the dialogue in order.

[1] BEN · ⁰ _*Were*_ (be) you at home yesterday?

[ ] BEN   Did they? ¹_____ (be) they good?

[ ] BEN   ²_____ (be) it a good party?

[ ] BEN   Oh, I remember. It ³_____ (be) your cousin's birthday yesterday, right?

[ ] SAM   Yes, they ⁴_____ (be) very good.

[ ] SAM   Yes, it ⁵_____ (be). I loved it.

[ ] SAM   Yes, it ⁶_____ (be). Her brothers are in a band. They ⁷_____ (play) at her party.

[ ] SAM   No, I ⁸_____ (not be). I ⁹_____ (be) at my cousin's house.

▰▰ TRAIN TO THiNK ▰▰

Sequencing

1 Complete the sequence with the words in the list.

And then
Finally
First

_____ > Then > _____ > After that > _____

2 Order the events in Rudyard Kipling's life. Then complete the sentences with sequencing words from Exercise 1.

Rudyard Kipling (1865–1936)
[ ] _____ he died in London in 1936.
[ ] _____ he lived in a seaside town in England with the Holloway family.
[1] _*First*_ Rudyard Kipling lived in India.
[ ] _____ he moved to a school in Devon.
[ ] _____ he moved back to India and he worked for a newspaper.

EXAM SKILLS: Listening

Listening for key words

1 🔊 40 **Listen and tick (✓) the months you hear.**

January ☐ | February ☐ | March ☐ | April ☐ | May ☐ | June ☐ | July ☐
August ☐ | September ☐ | October ☐ | November ☐ | December ☐

> ### Listening tip
> - First, learn to listen for key words, for example, the months of the year.
> - Next, you need to complete the profile. Listen carefully for the dates, the jobs and the places.
> **Remember!** You don't need to understand everything.

2 🔊 41 **Listen and ⟨circle⟩ the correct options to complete Claude Monet's profile.**

3 🔊 42 **Listen and complete Vincent Van Gogh's profile.**

Claude Monet

0 Job
writer / ⟨painter⟩

1 Nationality
French / Italian

2 Born
14th *September / November* 1840

3 Mother's job
singer / actor

4 Father's job
gardener / grocer

5 September 1870
He lived in *London / New York*.

6 May 1871
He moved to *Germany / Holland*.

7 May 1883
He moved to Giverny in *France / Belgium*.

8 Died
5th *June / December* 1926

Vincent Van Gogh

0 Job
painter

1 Nationality

2 Born

3 Studied

4 Moved to Paris

5 Lived with

6 Number of paintings sold when alive

7 Age died

8 Date died

9 Famous painting name

CONSOLIDATION

LISTENING

1 **◀)) 43** Listen to Susie and Jack and (circle) the correct answers (A, B or C).

1 For breakfast, Susie doesn't want …
   A orange juice.
   B cereal.
   C eggs.

2 Susie arrived home at …
   A eleven o'clock.
   B twelve o'clock.
   C one o'clock.

3 Susie wants to read her …
   A emails.
   B newspaper.
   C tablet.

2 **◀)) 43** Listen again. Mark the sentences T (true) or F (false).

1 Susie wants yoghurt for breakfast. ☐
2 She wants tea. ☐
3 Last night, Susie was at a party. ☐
4 Jack worked for five hours last night. ☐
5 Jack says he always works hard. ☐
6 The weather is rainy and cold. ☐
7 Susie wants to borrow Jack's tablet. ☐
8 Susie is going to work. ☐

GRAMMAR

3 (Circle) the correct options.

1 Mum, *can / must* I ask you a question?
2 Hurry up! We *must / mustn't* be late today.
3 Are you hungry? *Would / Do* you like a sandwich?
4 *It / There* wasn't a nice day yesterday. It was cold and rainy.
5 You really *can / must* be careful, John. Don't break it!
6 *Would / Do* you like this music?
7 *It / There* was a good film on TV last night.
8 Hi. *I like / I'd like* a cup of coffee, please.
9 My friend *wasn't / weren't* at school yesterday.
10 I *study / studied* for the test last night.

4 Complete the sentences with the correct form of the verbs in the list.

arrive | be (x2) | like | not be | rain
show (x2) | stay | travel | want | watch

Our holiday last year wasn't very good! We 1_____ to Scotland by car. We 2_____ very late and the man at the hotel 3_____ angry with us. Then he 4_____ us the rooms. They 5_____ really small and cold. We 6_____ to change the rooms but the man said that there 7_____ any other rooms. We 8_____ in the hotel for three days. The weather 9_____ good. It 10_____ almost all the time! One day we stayed in the room and 11_____ TV for about five hours. But the food was good. We 12_____ it a lot. Next year, we don't want to go to that hotel again.

VOCABULARY

5 Complete the words.

1 Do you want black coffee, or coffee with m _ _ k?
2 It's cold and w _ _ _ y today.
3 I don't eat a lot of v _ _ _ _ _ _ _ _ s.
4 My favourite fruit are o _ _ _ _ _ s.
5 I was at the cinema yesterday e _ _ _ _ _ g.
6 It was his birthday last m _ _ _ h.
7 There's no sun today – it's very c _ _ _ _ y.
8 I watched TV yesterday a _ _ _ _ _ _ _ n.
9 I'd like orange juice and eggs for b _ _ _ _ _ _ _ t.
10 I love eating b _ _ _ _ _ s and chips.

6 Complete the dialogue with the words in the list.

dinner | fruit | meat | night | o'clock
potatoes | strawberries | tea

TOM What time do you usually eat in your family?

NICKY Well, we usually have lunch at one 0 *o'clock* . And then we have 1_____ at eight in the evening.

TOM And what do you eat in the evening?

NICKY We have 2_____ – beef or chicken – and some vegetables, for example, carrots or 3_____ . I usually drink juice, but my parents like hot drinks, so they have 4_____ .

TOM And then?

NICKY Then we have 5_____ – usually bananas, but last 6_____ we had 7_____ , they're my favourite!

DIALOGUE

7 Complete the dialogue with the words in the list. There are two extra words.

bit | can | careful | course | liked | mustn't | thing | wanted | was | wasn't | were | weren't

NINA So, what was Jason's party like last night?

CRAIG It was good. We all enjoyed it. There ¹_____ great music and danced a lot. And all my friends were there.

NINA Was there any food?

CRAIG Yes. There ²_____ sandwiches and cheese, and some really nice chicken wings, too. The ³_____ is …

NINA Yes?

CRAIG Well, Jason's mum cooked some curry and it ⁴_____ good at all! No one ⁵_____ it. At the end of the party, it was all still there! I usually love curry, but not that!

NINA Oh, dear. Oh, look. Jason's coming. Be ⁶_____! We ⁷_____ say anything about the curry, OK?

CRAIG No, sure. Jason! Hi. How are you? Thanks for the party!

JASON Hi, Craig. Hi, Nina. No problem. I'm happy that you enjoyed it. But Craig, ⁸_____ I ask you something?

CRAIG Er, of ⁹_____. What?

JASON My mum's curry. Was it really terrible? No one ¹⁰_____ to eat it!

NINA Go on, Craig. I think you can tell him!

READING

8 Read Christie's diary entry. Then correct the sentences.

1 Yesterday was Christie's fourteenth birthday.

_____

2 The restaurant only serves Italian food.

_____

3 The restaurant was noisy.

_____

4 Christie didn't like the tomato soup.

_____

5 Christie's mother and father don't eat fish.

_____

6 Christie's family eat in restaurants a lot.

_____

7 There was writing on the candles.

_____

8 Christie's family is having dinner at a restaurant tonight.

_____

> March 17th
>
> Yesterday was my birthday so my family had dinner in a restaurant in town. It's an Italian restaurant, but they do all kinds of different food there. There weren't a lot of other people in the restaurant, so it was very quiet.
>
> The dinner was really nice. We started with tomato soup – it was delicious! Then I ordered beef with peppers and mushrooms. My parents ordered fish (they don't eat meat) with tomato sauce and rice.
>
> And after that, we had ice cream, my favourite. The food was really good – I enjoyed my meal a lot. We don't usually eat in restaurants so it was a special evening.
>
> When we finished the dinner, a waiter came over with a birthday cake! It had 13 candles on it (of course!) and 'Happy Birthday Christie' was in letters on the top of the cake. The waiters and my parents started to sing 'Happy Birthday to you' and the other people in the restaurant joined in, too. At the end of the song, everyone clapped – it was really nice! There was enough cake for us and for the other people in the restaurant, and there's some in the fridge in our kitchen now!
>
> So, dinner tonight at our house is pasta and salad – and birthday cake!

WRITING

9 Write a paragraph about a good or bad meal you remember. Write 35–50 words. Use the questions to help you.

- Where were you?
- What was the meal? (dinner? lunch?)
- Who was there?
- What was the food?
- Why was it a good/bad meal?

11 | A WORLD OF ANIMALS

GRAMMAR

Past simple: irregular verbs SB page 104

1 ★☆☆ **Complete the table with the past simple or the base form of the verbs.**

base form	past
0 ran	*ran*
1	came
2	put
3 give	
4 see	
5	knew
6	drank
7 fall	
8 write	
9	took
10 eat	

2 ★★☆ **Complete the text with the past simple form of the verbs in brackets.**

The Hill family's holiday

Last year the Hill family from Scotland decided to have a holiday in England. They ⁰___went___ (go) to the west of England. Mr Hill ¹_____ (make) a reservation at a hotel in Bath. In Bath they ²_____ (see) the Roman baths and the city centre. Then Pam ³_____ (find) Longleat Safari Park on her computer. She ⁴_____ (tell) her parents about the old house and the park with lions, gorillas and lots of different animals. The website ⁵_____ (say) it was the first safari park outside Africa. All the family ⁶_____ (think) it was a good idea. So they ⁷_____ (get) in the car and ⁸_____ (drive) to Longleat. They ⁹_____ (have) a really good time there!

Past simple (negative) SB page 104

3 ★★★ **Write sentences about a birthday party. Use the past simple negative.**

0 my grandmother / to the party (come)
   My grandmother didn't come to the party.

1 the band / classical music (play)

_____

2 we / bread and butter (eat)

_____

3 Sally / me a dictionary (give)

_____

4 Mum / my dress (make)

_____

5 Bob / a spider on the table (see)

_____

6 my father / us home (take)

_____

7 Steve / a snake in a box (find)

_____

8 we / a DVD (watch)

_____

4 ★★☆ **Larry didn't have a good weekend. Complete the sentences with the past simple form of the verbs in the list.**

be | be | decide | do | not do | not rain
not work | rain | try | use | want

0 Last weekend ___*was*___ awful.
1 It _____ all day on Saturday.
2 I _____ anything interesting.
3 I _____ to watch a film but the DVD player _____ .
4 My brother _____ the computer for his homework all afternoon.
5 I _____ to go out but it was too cold and wet.
6 But, it _____ on Sunday. Great!
7 So I _____ to ride my bike to the park.
8 But my bike _____ broken.
9 What _____ you _____ last weekend?

5 ★★★ Complete the text with the past simple form of the verbs in brackets.

Sarah ⁰ _____went_____ (go) to London last weekend with three friends. They stayed in a student hotel. It was very cheap, but the rooms ¹_____ (not be) very nice. Sarah ²_____ (share) a room with Lisa. The hotel has a café and on Friday evening they ³_____ (eat) supper there because they were tired from the journey. But Jason and Alex ⁴_____ (not like) the pizza very much. On Saturday morning, Sarah and Lucy ⁵_____ (go) to the Natural History Museum in South Kensington. They ⁶_____ (see) a dodo and a mammoth. Jason and Alex ⁷_____ (not want) to look at animals, so they ⁸_____ (spend) the morning in the Science Museum instead. In the evening they ⁹_____ (take) the tube to Leicester Square but they ¹⁰_____ (not watch) a film because all the cinemas were very expensive. So they ¹¹_____ (have) a pizza and this time the boys were happy!

Past simple (questions) `SB page 105`

6 ★★★ Use the information in Exercise 5 and write questions for these answers.

0
A *Where did Sarah go last weekend?*
B She went to London.

1
A Where _____
B In a hotel.

2
A What _____
   on Friday?
B A pizza in the café.

3
A What _____
B A dodo and a mammoth.

4
A Where _____
B In the Science Museum.

5
A What _____
B Pizza.

Pronunciation

Short vowel sound /ʊ/

Go to page 121. 🔊

---

could / couldn't `SB page 107`

7 ★★ Last year Brad broke his leg and they put it in plaster. What could he do? What couldn't he do? Use the phrases in the list.

do his homework | eat a pizza | go swimming
listen to music | ~~play football~~ | play the guitar
ride a bike | text his friends | ~~watch TV~~

0 *Billy could watch TV.* _____
0 *He couldn't play football.* _____
1 He _____
2 He _____
3 He _____
4 He _____
5 He _____
6 He _____
7 He _____

GET IT RIGHT! ⊙
Past simple

We always use the base form of the verb after *didn't* (in negative sentences) or *Did* (in questions).

✓ I **didn't go** to the party last Saturday.
✗ I ~~didn't went~~ to the party last Saturday.
✓ **Did** you **visit** the Science Museum?
✗ ~~Did you visited~~ the Science Museum.

Correct the sentences.

0 He didn't finished his homework.
   He didn't finish his homework.

1 Jack didn't liked the party.
   _____

2 We didn't paid much for lunch at the zoo yesterday.
   _____

3 Did they enjoyed their holiday?
   _____

4 We didn't knew where it was but finally we found it.
   _____

5 Bill's friend didn't ate a lot of food yesterday
   _____

6 Did you went to the party?
   _____

VOCABULARY

Word list

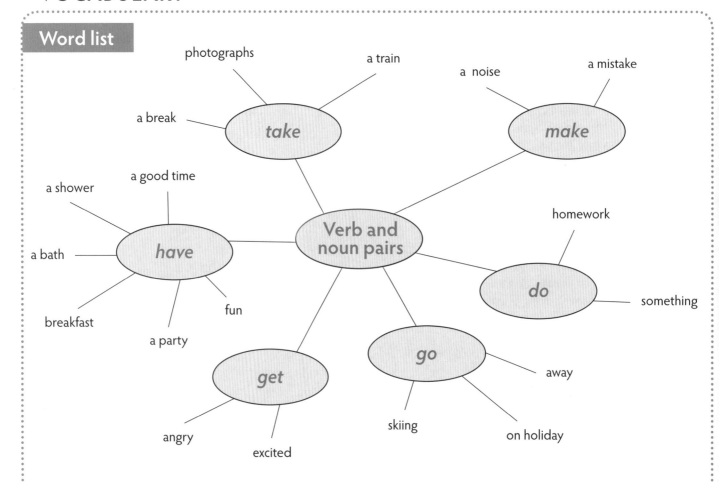

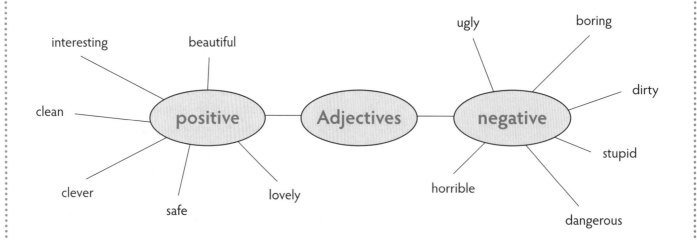

Key words in context

become	When she moved to France, my mum **became** a nurse.
extinct	There are no more dodos in the world. They are **extinct** now.
horn	Giraffes have got little **horns**.
island	Australia and Madagascar are very big **islands**.
ride	You can **ride** my new bicycle if you want to.
scared	I was **scared** because the dog was big and angry!
teeth	Birds haven't got **teeth**.
woods	It was very dark in the **woods** because there were a lot of trees.

Verb and noun pairs [SB page 104]

1 ★★ Read the sentences. Are the underlined words correct (✓) or incorrect (✗)? Write the correct words.

0   I always <u>do</u> my homework.   ✓

0   I <u>do</u> a shower every morning.   ✗
    have

1   I'm tired. Let's <u>take</u> a break now.   ☐

2   We just <u>went</u> the shopping for the party.   ☐

3   Try not to <u>do</u> a lot of mistakes.   ☐

4   Please don't <u>have</u> a noise when you come back.   ☐

5   We <u>made</u> some great photographs on holiday.   ☐

6   Did you <u>do</u> a good time at the party?   ☐

2 ★★ Complete the sentences with the correct verb in the correct form.

0   They ___*went*___ skiing last winter.

1   I always _____ excited the day before my birthday.

2   I always _____ something at the weekend. I never stay at home.

3   We live near an airport – the planes _____ a lot of noise every day.

4   Our weekend was fantastic! We _____ a party at our house.

5   Every day, when I wake up, I _____ a bath.

6   We weren't hungry so we didn't _____ breakfast.

7   _____ you always _____ the train to school?

Adjectives [SB page 107]

3 ★★ Unscramble the letters to make adjectives. Then look at the pictures and write the phrases.

0	1	2	3	4
ovllye	ercvel	tydri	putdis	regnoudas

0   *a lovely gorilla*   5   _____
1   _____   6   _____
2   _____   7   _____
3   _____   8   _____
4   _____   9   _____

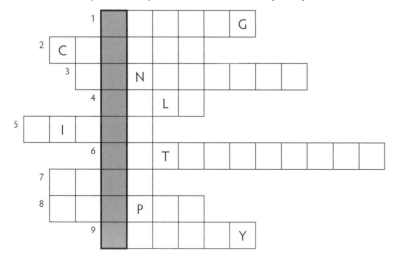

5	6	7	8	9
blehirro	gluy	teulauibf	tersniginet	lance

4 ★★ Complete the puzzle. What's the mystery word?

1 G
2 C
3 N
4 L
5 I
6 T
7
8 P
9 Y

1   I don't like this film, it's really _____ .

2   Cats are very _____ animals.

3   Bears can sometimes be _____ .

4   I don't like that house. I think it's _____ .

5   I have to wash my parents' car because it's very _____ .

6   The lesson today was great. It was really _____ .

7   Some big cities aren't very _____ at night.

8   Hey! That was a really _____ thing to do!

9   Thank you for my _____ birthday present.

Mystery word: _____

READING

1 [REMEMBER AND CHECK] (Circle) the correct answers (A, B or C). Then look at the article on page 103 of the Student's Book and check your answers.

0 Erin took a group of _____ people for a ride in the woods.

   A three   **B** fifteen   (C) eight

1 Erin's horse, Tonk, was _____ .

   A white   **B** black   **C** brown

2 The grizzly bear was _____ .

   A asleep   **B** angry   **C** scared

3 The boy's horse _____ .

   A stopped   **B** ran away   **C** jumped over a fence

4 The boy _____ .

   A fell off his horse   **B** jumped to the ground   **C** kicked his horse

5 Erin and Tonk ran at the bear _____ .

   A once   **B** twice   **C** three times

2 Read the stories. What are the dogs called? _____ _____

HERO DOGS

Story 1

Nick Lamb is 13 years old and he's deaf (he can't hear). He lives in Indianapolis, in the USA. He has a dog called Ace. One day, Nick was at home alone. His parents were at work. After lunch, Nick fell asleep in his room. Ace smelled fire in the house. He went into Nick's room, but Nick couldn't hear him, so he jumped on him to wake him up. Nick jumped up, covered his nose and mouth with his T-shirt and ran out of the house with Ace. Then he phoned the fire service and his mother. When the firefighters arrived, they could see the fire in the garage. No one was hurt.

Story 2

Roger Wilday is 68 years old and lives in Birmingham in England. One day, he went for a walk in a small park with his dog, Jade. Suddenly, Jade ran off into some trees. She didn't come back when Mr Wilday called her, so he went to find her. When he saw her, Jade was on the ground beside a plastic bag. Mr Wilday tried to move Jade, but he couldn't. Suddenly, Mr Wilday saw a small arm and heard a crying. There was a little baby in the bag! Mr Wilday called the police, who quickly took the baby to hospital. The nurse at the hospital said the baby was only about 24 hours old. The doctor said that the baby was lucky that the dog found her. The doctors called the baby 'Jade' and she's fine now.

3 Read the sentences and <u>underline</u> the incorrect information. Then write correct sentences.

Story 1

0 <u>Nick's mother</u> was at home alone.   *Nick was at home alone.*

1 Nick was in the garden.   _____

2 Nick covered his eyes and mouth.   _____

3 The fire was in the garden.   _____

Story 2

4 Mr Wilday went for a walk in the street with his dog.   _____

5 The dog ran into some flowers.   _____

6 Mr Wilday took the baby to hospital.   _____

7 The baby was about one week old.   _____

DEVELOPING WRITING

The life of an animal

1 Read the text. Which animal wrote it? Tick (✓) the correct animal.

Why we died out

We were great animals. We were very happy for a long time. We lived in a place that was a long way from the sea. It wasn't very warm, but that was OK. We could keep warm in the cold weather because we had thick coats.

But we had a serious problem. Other animals – we called them 'people' – wanted to kill us and eat us. Well, we didn't like that very much, of course. But we lived anyway.

And then, a long time ago, the weather changed. The days got hot. Our thick coats became a problem, and we couldn't live. Then, we died out.

dodo

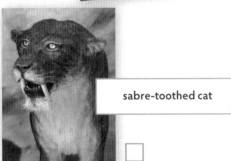

sabre-toothed cat

woolly rhinoceros

2 Complete the sentences with *but* or *because*.

1 We were happy, _____ there was a problem.
2 We weren't cold _____ we had thick coats.
3 It was cold _____ that was OK for us.
4 People killed us _____ they wanted to eat us.
5 We lived in a cold place _____ the weather started to change.
6 We died out _____ we couldn't live in the hot weather.

3 Look at the text in Exercise 1 and match the adjectives with the nouns.

1	thick	☐	a	weather
2	cold	☐	b	problem
3	great	☐	c	coat
4	serious	☐	d	animals

4 Choose one of the other two animals in the pictures. Look at the text on page 106 of the Student's Book and make notes about the animal in your notebook. Think about these questions.

● Where and when did it live?
● What was special about it?
● What could/couldn't it do?
● Why did it die out?

5 Use your notes in Exercise 4 and write a short text about the animal.

Why we died out

We were _____

We lived _____

We had _____

We could/couldn't _____

Then, _____

We died out because _____

LISTENING

1 🔊45 **Listen to Tommy and his granddad. What did Granddad have when he was young?**

cards ☐
computers ☐
envelopes ☐
Internet ☐
letters ☐
mobile phones ☐
paper ☐
pens ☐

2 🔊45 **Listen again. Mark the sentences T (true) or F (false).**

0	Tommy went in a time machine.	F
1	The professor made a time machine.	☐
2	The time machine went back ten years.	☐
3	The kids saw a dodo.	☐
4	Granddad had a computer fifty years ago.	☐
5	He had a phone.	☐
6	He could walk around with his phone.	☐
7	Granddad didn't use a computer to do his homework.	☐
8	Tommy thinks life was simple then.	☐

DIALOGUE

1 **Complete the dialogue with the words and phrases in the list.**

after that | and | because | but | Poor you | Then

BARBARA Did you have a good weekend?

KEN Yes it was great, thanks. I went to Miguel's party.

BARBARA Oh, right. He invited me too, 0 _but_ I couldn't go.

KEN Why not?

BARBARA My aunt and uncle were here for the weekend 1_____ they wanted to take us out.

KEN That's nice. Where did you go?

BARBARA We went to the theatre. It was really boring.

KEN 2_____ !

BARBARA But 3_____ we went and had pizza. That was good! 4_____ I ordered an enormous ice cream. I couldn't eat it all, I was so full.

KEN That's like me at the party. I couldn't dance 5_____ I was really tired from football on Saturday!

2 **Read the dialogue again and answer the questions.**

1 Why couldn't Barbara go to the party?

_____

2 Why couldn't Barbara eat all the ice cream?

_____

3 Why couldn't Ken dance at the party?

_____

PHRASES FOR FLUENCY

SB page 109

1 **Unscramble the letters to make expressions.**

0 dunylsed   _suddenly_

1 lal thrig.   _____

2 opor oyu.   _____

3 thwa phedapen?   _____

2 **Complete the dialogue with the expressions in Exercise 1.**

ANNIE Do you know what happened to me last weekend?

KATE No, of course not. I wasn't with you last weekend. 0 _What happened?_

ANNIE 1_____ , I'll tell you. On Saturday, I was in the café in the High Street, and 2_____ someone waved at me!

KATE So? Who was it?

ANNIE It was Jenny Hall.

KATE Jenny Hall? Are you sure? Jenny's in the USA! She went last year.

ANNIE Well, she's here on holiday. But it was awful.

KATE Why?

ANNIE I couldn't remember her name! I called her Sally. And she got really angry with me! She shouted at me!

KATE Oh, 3_____ I'm sure that was horrible for you!

Sum it up

TIME-O-TRON TRAVEL

See the dinosaurs!

Talk to William Shakespeare!

Watch the Egyptians building the pyramids!

Welcome to the wonderful world of Time-O-Tron Travel.

As you know, last year the famous Professor Godbole of Delhi University invented the
Time-O-Tron Travel Machine

Now, you can go into the past! (Sorry, no future travel yet – maybe next year?)

Sit in the **Time-O-Tron**, choose your time in the past – and whoosh! Off you go!

We are offering one-day trips into the past for only US$1,000,000! That's right! Only a million dollars for 24 hours in a past time that you choose.

But here's some really good news – we have a competition and the five winners will get a free one-day trip in the **Time-O-Tron**!

All you have to do is write to say what time in the past you want to travel to, and why. Write between 10 and 20 words, beginning with 'I want to go to …' Here are two examples to help you.

'I want to go to pre-history and see the dinosaurs because they're fantastic animals!' (Monika, Germany)

'I want to go to 1998 because that's when my country won the World Cup, but I wasn't alive then!' (Pierre, France)

But remember – if you win, you must go to the time you wrote about!

GOOD LUCK!

Send your ideas to us at: Time-O-Tron Travel, P.O. Box 2020, London

1 **Read the advertisement. Mark the sentences T (true) or F (false).**

1 A man in New York invented the travel machine. ☐
2 You can travel to the past and into the future. ☐
3 You can buy a trip into the past for a million US dollars. ☐
4 The time trips are for one day. ☐
5 Five people can win a prize in the competition. ☐
6 If you win, you can go to any past time that you want. ☐

2 **Imagine there's a time machine! Where would you like to go? Write an entry for the competition.**

- Say what time in the past you want to travel to, and why.
- Write a paragraph, beginning with 'I want to go to …'

GRAMMAR
Comparative adjectives
SB page 112

1 ★☆☆ <u>Underline</u> the comparative adjective in each sentence.

0 The train is <u>quicker</u> than the car.
1 His computer is more expensive than my computer.
2 Surfing is more dangerous than ice skating.
3 The weather in winter is worse than in summer.
4 Spanish is easier than English.
5 Your photo is better than my photo.
6 My house is further from school than your house.
7 Salad is healthier than hot dogs.
8 Their car is bigger than our car.

2 ★☆☆ Complete the table with the correct adjective forms.

	Adjective	Comparative
0	dirty	*dirtier*
1	beautiful	
2	cold	
3		curlier
4	hot	
5		cleaner
6		shorter
7	ugly	
8		more boring
9	sad	
10	warm	
11	lovely	
12		slower
13		more interesting

3 ★★☆ Look at the table and mark the sentences T (true) or F (false). Correct the false sentences.

	Leaves Glasgow	Arrives London	Price
train	8 am	1 pm	£140
bus	5 am	5 pm	£35
plane	10 am	11.30 am	£70

0 The bus is cheaper than the train. `T`

1 The bus arrives later than the train. ☐

2 The bus is slower than the plane. ☐

3 The bus is more expensive than the plane. ☐

4 The plane is faster than the train. ☐

5 The plane arrives earlier than the train. ☐

4 ★★★ Use the table in Exercise 3 to write sentences. Use comparative adjectives.

0 bus / early / train
  The bus is earlier than the train.
1 train / fast / bus
  _____
2 plane / expensive / bus
  _____
3 train / slow / plane
  _____
4 plane / late / bus
  _____
5 bus / cheap / train
  _____

Pronunciation
Word stress – comparatives
Go to page 121. 🔊

5 ★★★ Look at the pictures and write sentences to compare the two taxi companies. Use the adjectives in the list to help you.

big | clean | dangerous | dirty | expensive | fast | good | safe

0   *Linda's Limos are cleaner than Tom's taxis.*

1   _____

2   _____

3   _____

4   _____

5   _____

6   _____

7   _____

6 ★★★ Complete the sentences so they are true for you.

1   I'm _____ than my parents.

2   My best friend is _____ than me.

3   English lessons are _____ than Maths lessons.

4   Dogs are _____ than cats.

5   Summer is _____ than winter.

6   Cars are _____ than trains.

one / ones   **SB page 115**

7 ★   (Circle) the correct options.

0   Can I have a look at those shoes? The *one /* (*ones*) in the window.

1   Don't make me a sandwich. I don't want *one / ones*.

2   I like most films but I don't like *one / ones* about war.

3   I can't give you a pen because I haven't got *one / ones*.

4   I've got some chocolates. Would you like *one / ones*?

5   I'm interested in cars and I really like Italian *one / ones*.

8 ★★   Write *one* into the dialogues.

0   A   Where's your house?
   B   My house is the first ˅*one* on the left.

1   A   How was your birthday?
   B   Great. I got lots of presents, but my favourite was a book from my dad.

2   A   Which dress did you buy?
   B   Well, I love blue so I bought the blue.

3   A   How is your new computer?
   B   It's faster than my old and it's easier to use.

4   A   Is that your brother over there?
   B   Yes, he's the with the glasses.

GET IT RIGHT! 👁

one and *ones*

We use *one* or *ones* after an adjective when we want to avoid repeating a noun.

✓ *I like this song, it's a good **one**.*

✗ *I like this song, it's a good song.*

✓ *I wore my new shoes – the red **ones**.*

✗ *I wore my new shoes – the red shoes.*

Replace one of the nouns with *one* or *ones*.

0   How much are the cakes? I like the big cakes.
   How much are the cakes? I like the big ones.

1   These tickets are expensive. We can find cheaper tickets.
   _____

2   This pen isn't good. I've got a better pen in my bag.
   _____

3   The black jeans are too big. The blue jeans are much better.
   _____

4   All of the buses go there but the green bus is the fastest.
   _____

5   Where are my black shoes? They were next to my red shoes.
   _____

VOCABULARY

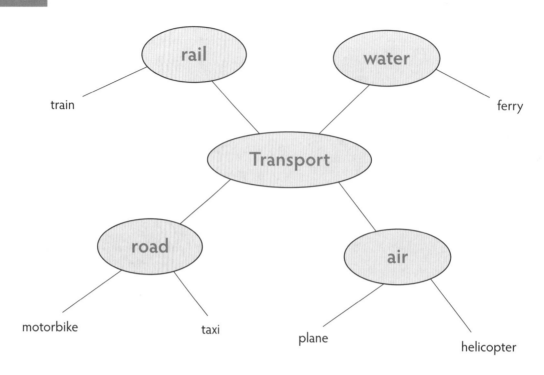

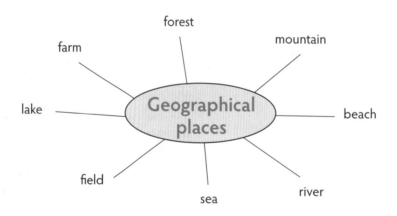

Key words in context

airport	The plane arrives at the **airport** at 10 pm.
journey	The **journey** from my house to school is about ten minutes.
medal	The winner of the race gets a **medal**.
platform	The London train leaves from **platform** 12.
pollute	Cars **pollute** the air.
presenter	My mum's a TV **presenter**. She presents the news.
return	A **return** is for the journey there and back.
side	The train is over there on the other **side** of the bridge.
single	A **single** is for the journey there.
ticket	You need a **ticket** to travel on the bus.
traffic	There's a lot of **traffic** in our town. It's terrible for drivers.

Transport SB page 112

1 ★ Find and (circle) six types of transport in the word snake.

gemotorbikeasehelicopternmbdplanerkutaxilfqferryipatrainbgh

2 ★★ Unscramble the column titles and complete the table with words from Exercise 1.

no het ardo	no sairl	ni eth ria	no tware
0 *on the road*	1	2	3
motorbike			

3 ★★★ Match the words in Exercise 1 with the definitions.

0 It flies in the air but it doesn't have wings. *helicopter*

1 It travels on rails and is very long. _____

2 It flies in the air. It has wings. _____

3 It travels on water and carries a lot of people. _____

4 You pay someone to drive you. _____

5 It drives on the road but only has two wheels. _____

Geographical places SB page 115

4 ★★ Find the places in the word search.

Q	F	D	N	U	B	W	W	M
H	E	E	O	E	G	S	O	S
F	V	S	A	D	R	U	E	E
O	M	C	D	U	N	A	K	R
R	H	R	R	T	B	A	E	U
E	T	P	A	B	L	V	S	C
S	X	I	E	F	I	P	B	T
T	N	C	K	R	R	T	D	B
Z	D	L	E	I	F	L	O	V

5 ★★ Match the geographical places with the famous examples.

1 mountain ☐
2 lake ☐
3 river ☐
4 beach ☐
5 sea ☐

a The Nile, The Amazon, The Yangtze

b Aconcagua, K2, Kilimanjaro

c Copacabana, Bondi, Kuta

d Caspian, Mediterranean, Red

e Michigan, Titicaca, Victoria

6 ★★★ Complete the sentences with examples from your own country.

1 My favourite beach is

_____ .

2 The highest mountain is

_____ .

3 A famous lake is _____ .

4 The longest river is _____ .

5 _____ is a good place to go on holiday.

6 _____ is a beautiful place in the summer / winter.

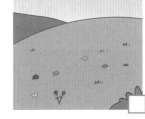

READING

1 **REMEMBER AND CHECK** Mark the sentences T (true) or F (false). Then look at the article on page 111 of the Student's Book and check your answers.

0 Walking is the best way to make a short journey in London. `T`

1 The presenters made a 27 km journey in London. ☐

2 One of the presenters walked. ☐

3 The speedboat was faster than public transport. ☐

4 The presenters were unhappy the bike won. ☐

5 The presenters decided that the car won. ☐

2 Read the blog. Which of these types of transport is <u>not</u> mentioned?

☐ ☐ ☐ ☐ ☐ ☐

Racing around the world!

My favourite book is called *Around the World in 80 Days*. It's the story of a man who makes a bet that he can travel the planet in less than 80 days. Of course, these days that's not difficult, but the book is set more than 100 years ago. I love the idea of adventure and exploring, so it's no surprise that my favourite TV program is called *The Amazing Race*. It's an American game show and it's really exciting. In the show, teams race against each other around the world to win a big prize. There are two people in each team, for example: a husband and wife, a father and son, best friends, etc. It's important that they have a good relationship because the race is really difficult and they need to be strong and help each other.

The race takes them all over the world and they use lots of different types of transport. They use planes, of course, to make the longer journeys but they also use boats, taxis, buses, helicopters, bikes, cars, trains; any transport that makes their journey quicker.

At the beginning of each show, the presenter gives the teams ideas about where they have to go. The last team to arrive at that place leaves the show. When there are only three teams left they race to the final place. The team that arrives first usually wins lots of money.

I love this show because you see lots of really exciting places all over the world. One day I want to be on the show.

3 Read the blog again and match the sentence halves.

0 *Around the World in 80 Days* `g`

1 *The Amazing Race* ☐

2 The race is ☐

3 The people in the teams ☐

4 The teams race ☐

5 The teams use ☐

6 The last team to arrive ☐

7 In the final ☐

8 The winning team ☐

a between teams of two people.

b all over the world.

c leaves the show.

d gets lots of money.

e is a TV show from the US.

f lots of different types of transport.

g is a famous book.

h know each other.

i there are three teams.

4 Do you want to be on *The Amazing Race*? Why/Why not? Write a short paragraph (35–50 words).

DEVELOPING WRITING

Writing about a journey

1 Read about Eric and Dawn's favourite journey and complete the table.

	from	to	transport	time it takes	why I like it
Eric					
Dawn					

Eric

My favourite journey is the one I do every Sunday morning to play football. I leave my house at about ten o'clock and get on my bike to cycle the two kilometres to the park. It takes me about 15 minutes. At the park I meet my friends and we play football for two hours. Then I get on my bike and ride back home. I like the journey there because I get excited about playing football. I don't like the journey back so much because I'm usually quite tired. But when I have a good game, the journey back is great, too, because I think about the game.

Dawn

The journey I like best is the one from my house to the airport. My dad lives in Greece and three times every year I fly there to spend some time with him. The journey starts really early. The taxi picks me up from my house at 4 am! But that's OK, because I'm always really happy. It's only 30 minutes to the airport but I can't wait to get there. The plane journey is about four hours. It's OK, but I'm usually a bit nervous about flying. My dad always meets me at the airport and then he drives me to his house. We don't stop talking the whole journey. I never like the journey back. I'm always really sad to leave.

2 Read the texts again and complete the sentences.

0   Eric likes his journey to the park because *he gets excited about playing football.*

1   He doesn't like the journey back because _____

2   Dawn likes the journey to the airport because _____

3   She doesn't like the journey back because _____

3 Make notes to complete the table so it is true for you.

	from	to	transport	time	why I like it
Me					

4 Use your notes to write a text about your favourite journey. Write 35–50 words.

My favourite journey is _____

_____

_____

_____

_____

_____

LISTENING

1 🔊47 **Listen to the dialogue. Where is Jill? Who is she talking to?**

_____

2 🔊47 **Listen again and ⟨circle⟩ the correct answers (A, B or C).**

0 Where does Jill want to go?

  A Central London

  Ⓑ Liverpool

  C Manchester

1 What time is the next train?

  A

  B

  C

2 How often is there a train?

  A every 15 minutes

  B every 30 minutes

  C every 50 minutes

3 How long is the journey?

  A 40 minutes

  B 35 minutes

  C 45 minutes

4 When is Jill returning?

  A today

  B tomorrow

  C at the weekend

5 How much is the ticket?

  A £7.80

  B £8.70

  C £17.80

6 What platform is the train leaving from?

  A 3

  B 4

  C 5

7 What time does Jill get the train?

  A

  B

  C

DIALOGUE

1 **⟨Circle⟩ the correct options. Then put the dialogue in order.**

☐	ASSISTANT	The journey is three ¹_quarters / halves_ of an hour.
☐	ASSISTANT	OK, that's £5.50, please.
☐	ASSISTANT	Platform 5. Have a ²_good / boring_ journey.
☐	ASSISTANT	Let me see. There's a train every 15 minutes so the next one is at half past three.
☐	ASSISTANT	Do you want a single or a return?
1	ASSISTANT	Good afternoon. ³_How / Who_ can I help you?
☐	WOMAN	That's great. And how long does it take?
☐	WOMAN	Thank you.
☐	WOMAN	I want to ⁴_go / come_ to Liverpool. What time's the next train?
☐	WOMAN	Just one more thing. What platform does the train leave ⁵_from / at_?
☐	WOMAN	45 minutes. That's quick. Can I have a ticket, please?
☐	WOMAN	Return, please. I'm coming back later.

▰▰ TRAIN TO THiNK ▰▰

Comparing

1 **Complete the diagram with the words in the list. Then use your own ideas and write six more words.**

boring | dangerous | exciting | expensive | fun | relaxing

Holidays by the sea

Holidays in the mountains

2 **Write sentences to compare the two different types of holidays in Exercise 1.**

_____

_____

_____

EXAM SKILLS: Reading and Writing

Answering open cloze questions

1   Read Danny's answers in the exam task below. How many did he get right? How many did he get wrong?

Complete the text about travelling to and from school. Write ONE word for each space.

I live **(0)** .... in ...... a small town and my school is about eight kilometres away. Most days I take the school bus. It stops outside my house **(1)** ...... at ...... 7.30 every morning. In the summer when the weather **(2)** ..... are ..... good, I usually cycle to school. It's quicker **(3)** .... than .... the bus because the bus stops all the time. The problem with the bike is when my school bag is too heavy. Then it's **(4)** ..... not ..... fun.

Sometimes I wake up late and **(5)** ..... mis ..... the school bus. Mum takes me to school **(6)** ...... in ...... the car. She doesn't like this **(7)** .. because .. she needs to get to work, too. Once I missed the bus home and I had to **(8)** .... tired .... home. It took me more than **(9)** .. half an .. hour to walk. I don't want **(10)** ...... to ...... do that again.

> ### Reading and writing tip
>
> - Read the instructions carefully. Underline the key words. Words like circle, tick, choose and underline tell you how to complete the question. Look for other important information, for example, *Only write one word*.
> - When you have finished, read your answers again. Have you followed the instructions? Have you used the correct type of word (verb, noun, adjective, etc.)? Have you used the singular and plural forms correctly? Is your spelling correct?
> - Don't leave any gaps. If you don't know the answer, guess!

2   Put Danny's mistakes under the correct heading. Write the number.

Used more than one word	Used the wrong type of word (adjective instead of verb)	Used singular and plural forms incorrectly	Used incorrect spelling
9			

3   Correct Danny's mistakes. Write the correct words next to the numbers in Exercise 2.

4   Complete the text about favourite holidays. Write ONE word for each space.

My favourite holidays **(0)** ..... are ..... beach holidays. I like the sun **(1)** .... the sea. I usually go on beach holidays **(2)** .... the summer with my family. Sometimes Dad drives and sometimes we **(3)** .... the train. Last year we went **(4)** .... holiday in the countryside. We stayed on **(5)** .... farm. There was a river and a lake and lots **(6)** .... fields, too. It was OK but I prefer beach holidays. The weather by the sea is usually hotter **(7)** .... in the countryside. Dad wants to **(8)** .... on holiday in the mountains this year. I'm **(9)** .... happy about that idea. I don't want another year away **(10)** .... the beach.

CONSOLIDATION

LISTENING

1 🔊48 Listen to Arnie and (circle) the correct answers (A, B or C).

1 How old is Arnie's brother?
   A eight   B nine   C ten
2 At the zoo, which animals scared Arnie's brother?
   A the elephants B the lions   C the tigers
3 How many jaguars were there?
   A two   B three   C four

2 🔊48 Listen again and answer the questions.

1 Why did Arnie's family go to the zoo?

_____

2 Who took photographs at the zoo?

_____

3 What was Arnie happy about?

_____

4 What did Arnie think about the visit to the zoo?

_____

5 Why was Arnie sorry for the jaguars?

_____

6 What two things does Arnie think zoo animals need?

_____

GRAMMAR

3 Complete the sentences with the correct form of the words in brackets.

1 Yesterday I _____ some money on the street in town. (find)
2 For my last birthday, my parents _____ me tickets for a concert. (give)
3 My friends and I _____ to the cinema three times last weekend. (go)
4 I arrived home late last night but I _____ any noise. (not make)
5 Yesterday's test was _____ than the one on Friday. (difficult)
6 _____ you _____ that film on TV last Sunday night? (see)
7 The weather today is _____ than yesterday. (bad)
8 I practise a lot and I'm getting _____ every day! (good)
9 I _____ many presents for my birthday. (not get)
10 Are tigers _____ than jaguars? (big)

VOCABULARY

4 (Circle) the odd one out in each list. Explain your reasons.

0 safe   clean   (homework)
   a noun – the other two are adjectives
1 motorbike   plane   helicopter

2 shopping   homework   a mistake

3 forest   sea   lake

4 train   river   underground

5 a break   a good time photographs

6 boat   ferry   taxi

7 a mistake   a shower   a noise

8 breakfast   elephant   horse

9 field   beach   farm

5 Use a word or phrase from Exercise 4 to complete each sentence.

1 Shh! Don't make _____ or that pretty bird will fly away.
2 We went for a walk in the _____ this morning. The trees were very beautiful.
3 My mum doesn't like me riding my bike in the city. She thinks it isn't _____ .
4 This party's great. I'm having _____ .
5 Her name's Julie but I made _____ and called her Jenny.
6 I like having _____ after football to get clean again!
7 We went to the beach but I didn't swim in the _____ – I think it's dangerous.
8 I'm really tired. Let's take _____ and have some coffee.

DIALOGUE

6 Complete the dialogue with the words and phrases in the list. There are two extra words.

All right | better | came | cheaper | could | couldn't | Did | lovely | made | Poor you | suddenly | What happened

MIKE   How was your weekend at the beach?

MARIA   Oh, awful. Everything went wrong.

MIKE   Oh, dear. ¹_____ ?

MARIA   Well, first, we missed the train.

MIKE   But you got there in the end?

MARIA   Oh, yes, we got there. We always stay at the same hotel. But it's very expensive, so this year
         Dad said: 'Let's stay at a ²_____ hotel.' I said, 'Dad! If our usual hotel is more expensive,
         that's because it's ³_____ than the cheaper ones.' ⁴_____ he listen? No, he didn't.
         The hotel was horrible! I ⁵_____ sleep at all – there were cars outside all night. They
         ⁶_____ a lot of noise!

MIKE   ⁷_____ , but what about the beach?

MARIA   The beach there is really ⁸_____ . We like it a lot. So we went there on the first day – but
         ⁹_____ , it started to rain! We ¹⁰_____ home a day early. The weekend was … well,
         it was horrible.

READING

The Lake District – there's nowhere more beautiful!

Are you thinking about taking a break? Then think about going to the Lake District. This lovely part of England has mountains, forests, rivers – and, of course, lakes! There aren't many more beautiful lakes in the world than Lake Windermere or Lake Grasmere and the others.
Some lakes have boat trips. You spend an hour or two in the sun (in summer, anyway!) as you travel slowly along the lake.
There are small market towns like Ambleside and Windermere. Some of the shops there are more expensive than the ones you see in the big towns and cities, but they're different and also much nicer. These small towns are safe, clean and very nice to visit.
The Lake District has lots of hotels and small bed-and-breakfast places. The B&B places are cheaper but sometimes they're as good as hotels, or even more comfortable!
It's easy to get to the Lake District. Trains from London to Windermere take about three hours. From Manchester it's even quicker: it's only one or two hours from there.
So, think about visiting the Lake District. We're looking forward to seeing you here!

7 Read the web page. Mark the sentences T (true) or F (false).

1 There are forests in the Lake District. ☐

2 Lake Windermere and Lake Grasmere aren't in the Lake District. ☐

3 It's possible to travel by boat on some of the lakes. ☐

4 Ambleside is a big town. ☐

5 You find the same shops in the Lake District that you find in
   big towns and cities. ☐

6 The small towns in the Lake District are a bit dirty. ☐

7 Hotels there are more expensive than B&B places. ☐

WRITING

8 Write a paragraph about a nice area that you know. Use the questions to help you. Write 35–50 words.

● What is it called?

● What are the good things about it?

● What can people do there?

● How can you get there?

PRONUNCIATION

UNIT 1
/h/ or /w/ in question words

1 Look at the question words. Two of them start with the /h/ sound and the others start with the /w/ sound. Write /h/ or /w/ next to the words.

0 Why   _/w/_
1 How   _____
2 Where   _____
3 Who   _____
4 What   _____
5 When   _____

2 🔊 10 Listen, check and repeat.

3 Match the words that sound the same.

0	Why		a	now
1	How		b	got
2	Where		c	chair
3	Who		d	then
4	What		e	I
5	When		f	you

4 🔊 11 Listen, check and repeat.

UNIT 2
Vowel sounds – adjectives

1 🔊 13 Listen and repeat the adjectives.

angry	awful	bored	busy
friendly	funny	happy	hot
hungry	sad	thirsty	worried

2 Complete the table with the words in Exercise 1.

a (cat)	e (get)	i (six)	o (dog)
0 _angry_	3	4	5
1			
2			

u (bus)	or (for)	ir (bird)	
6	9	11	
7	10		
8			

3 🔊 14 Listen, check and repeat.

UNIT 3
this / that / these / those

1 🔊 17 Listen and repeat. Then look at the underlined sounds and (circle) the odd sound out.

0	those	go	home	bored
1	that	sad	late	have
2	them	these	please	meet
3	give	like	this	sing
4	hot	cold	know	those
5	wife	this	nice	exciting
6	these	she	get	we
7	famous	that	family	happy

2 🔊 17 Listen again, check and repeat.

UNIT 4
Word stress in numbers

1 🔊19 **Listen to the words and write them in the correct column according to the stress.**

~~eighteen~~ | ~~eighty~~ | forty | fourteen | nineteen
ninety | sixteen | sixty | thirty | thirteen

oO	Oo
eighteen	*eighty*

2 🔊19 **Listen again, check and repeat.**

UNIT 5
Present simple verbs – 3rd person

1 **Complete the table with the correct present simple third person singular form of the verbs in the list.**

~~catch~~ | ~~cook~~ | choose | dance | help | look
sing | teach | walk | wash | watch | wish | work

One syllable	Two syllables
cooks	*catches*

2 🔊23 **Listen, check and repeat.**

UNIT 6
Long vowel sound /eɪ/

1 🔊25 **Listen to these words. They all contain the /eɪ/ sound. <u>Underline</u> the sound in each word.**

0   br<u>ea</u>k
1   eight
2   face
3   great
4   grey
5   make
6   rainy
7   say
8   straight
9   take
10 they
11 waiter

2 **Complete the sentences with the words in Exercise 1.**

0   How do you _____*say*_____ that word in English?

1   Is your grandmother the woman with the wavy _____ hair?

2   Let's _____ Clara a friendship band for her birthday!

3   My little sister is _____ years old.

4   These are my friends. _____ like playing football with me.

5   It's _____ today. Let's go to the cinema.

6   My father's a _____ at that restaurant.

7   I brush my teeth and wash my _____ every morning.

8   I like playing tennis. It's a _____ game!

9   Can you _____ this book to your teacher? Thank you.

10 My hair's _____ but my best friend's hair is curly.

11 Put your books away. It's time for a _____ .

3 🔊26 **Listen, check and repeat.**

UNIT 7
Long vowel sound /ɔː/

1   🔊29 **Listen to these words. They all contain the /ɔː/ sound. Underline the sound in each word.**

   0   A<u>u</u>gust
   1   autumn
   2   daughter
   3   door
   4   forty
   5   important
   6   quarter
   7   short
   8   snowboarding
   9   sport
   10 walk
   11 water

2   **Complete the sentences with the words in Exercise 1.**

   0   Please close the ___*door*___ when you go out.
   1   It's a beautiful day. Let's go for a _____ .
   2   In _____ the leaves change to orange and it gets colder.
   3   English is a very _____ language.
   4   My birthday's on the fourth of _____ .
   5   The tall girl with the curly hair is my teacher's _____ .
   6   Jenny likes _____ in the mountains in winter.
   7   My favourite _____ is volleyball.
   8   I'm thirsty. Can I have a glass of _____ , please?
   9   My hair is long but my friend's is _____ .
   10 My first class at school starts at _____ to nine in the morning.
   11 It's my father's birthday today. He's _____ years old.

3   🔊30 **Listen, check and repeat.**

UNIT 8
Intonation – listing items

1   **Complete the lists. Then draw a ↑ and a ↓ to show where intonation rises and falls in each list.**

arm | Brazil | catch | coat | cooker | headphones
library | Russian | rugby | J̶u̶n̶e̶ | spring | wife

      ↑   ↑   ↑   ↓

   0   March, April, May and ___*June*___
   1   son, daughter, husband and _____
   2   Japanese, British, _____ and Turkish
   3   _____ , skirt, socks and trousers
   4   snowboarding, gymnastics, golf and _____
   5   summer, _____ , winter and autumn
   6   watch, choose, throw and _____
   7   _____ , shower, fridge and armchair
   8   Australia, Scotland, _____ and Japan
   9   body, _____ , leg and face
   10 tablet, GPS, _____ and laptop
   11 _____ , restaurant, museum and bank

2   🔊32 **Listen, check and repeat.**

UNIT 9
Intonation – giving two choices

1 🔊36 **Complete the dialogue with the words in the list. Then listen and check.**

chicken | chips | fish | ice cream
pineapple | ~~soup~~ | tea | water

	↑	↓

WAITER   Would you like salad or ⁰ _soup_ ?

WOMAN   Salad, please.

	☐	☐

WAITER   Chicken or ¹ _____ ?

WOMAN   I think I'll have ² _____ today –
with ³ _____ , please.

WAITER   Would you like dessert?

WOMAN   Yes, please.

	☐	☐

WAITER   Cake or ⁴ _____ ?

WOMAN   I'd prefer fruit – some ⁵ _____ ,
please.

WAITER   Would you like something to drink?

WOMAN   Yes, please – just some ⁶ _____ .
And a cup of ⁷ _____ after the
meal. Thank you.

2 🔊36 **Draw ↑ or ↓ above the waiter's questions.
Then listen, check and repeat.**

UNIT 10
Past simple regular verbs

1 **Say the verbs in the list in the past tense and
decide if they are one syllable or two. Then write
the verbs in the correct column.**

~~dance~~ | ~~hate~~ | help | like | live | need
play | start | wait | walk | want | work

One syllable	Two syllables
danced	_hated_

2 🔊38 **Listen, check and repeat.**

3 **Complete the rule.**

We only say /ɪd/ when the final sound in the word is a
/ _____ / or a / _____ /.

UNIT 11
Short vowel sound /ʊ/

1 ⬭Circle⬭ **the odd sound out.**

0	cook	cool	food
1	house	shout	could
2	June	put	who
3	room	you	woods
4	pull	fun	son
5	foot	full	jump
6	move	zoo	good
7	funny	woolly	sunny
8	school	room	book
9	push	run	bus
10	cousin	couldn't	country

2 🔊44 **Listen, check and repeat.**

UNIT 12
Word stress – comparatives

1 **Write the comparative form of the adjectives.
Underline the stressed syllable.**

0	slow	_slower_	8	big	_____
1	small	_____	9	hot	_____
2	quick	_____	10	funny	_____
3	cheap	_____	11	easy	_____
4	fast	_____	12	healthy	_____
5	cold	_____	13	happy	_____
6	safe	_____	14	far	_____
7	close	_____	15	good	_____

2 🔊46 **Listen, check and repeat.**

3 **Complete the rule.**

When adding -er to make a comparative, the *first* / *second*
syllable is always stressed.

GRAMMAR REFERENCE

UNIT 1
Question words

1   **Questions that begin with *Who* ask about a person / people.**

    Who is he?
    He's the new teacher.

2   **Questions that begin with *What* ask about a thing / things.**

    What's that?
    It's a mobile phone.

3   **Questions that begin with *When* ask about a time / day / year / etc.**

    When's the football match?
    It's at three o'clock.

4   **Questions that begin with *Where* ask about a place.**

    Where's Cambridge?
    It's in the UK.

5   **Questions that begin with *Why* ask for a reason.**

    Why are you here?
    Because I want to see you.

6   **Questions that begin with *How old* ask about age.**

    How old is she?
    She's sixteen.

to be

1   **The present simple of *to be* is like this:**

Singular	Plural
I am	we are
you are	you are
he/she/it is	they are

2   **In speaking and informal writing we use contracted (short) forms.**

    I'm, you're, he's, she's, it's, we're, they're

    I'm from Russia.

    She's late.

    We're hungry.

UNIT 2
to be (negative, singular and plural)

1   We make the verb *to be* negative by adding *not*.

Singular	Plural
I am not (I'm not)	we are not (we aren't)
you are not (you aren't)	you are not (you aren't)
he/she/it is not (he/she/it isn't)	they are not (they aren't)

I'm not Brazilian. I'm Portuguese.
He isn't late. He's early!
They aren't from Spain. They're from Mexico.

to be (questions and short answers)

To make questions with *to be*, we put the verb before the subject. We make short answers with *Yes* or *No* + subject + the verb *to be*. We don't use contracted forms in positive short answers (NOT: *Yes, you're*.)

Am I late?	Yes, you are. / No, you aren't.
Are you American?	Yes, I am. / No, I'm not.
Is he a singer?	Yes, he is. / No, he isn't.
Is she from Japan?	Yes, she is. / No, she isn't.
Are we right?	Yes, we are. / No, we aren't.
Are they French?	Yes, they are. / No, they aren't.

Object pronouns

1   **Object pronouns come after a verb. We use them instead of nouns.**

    I like the film. I like it.
    I love my sister. I love her.
    They are friends with you and me. They are friends with us.
    I like the girls at my school. I like them.

2   **The object pronouns are:**

Subject	I	you	he	she	it	we	they
Object	me	you	him	her	it	us	them

UNIT 3
Possessive 's

1 We use 's after a noun to say who something belongs to.

Dad's room
John's car
Sandra's family
the cat's bed
my brother's friend
your sister's school

2 We don't usually say ~~the room of Dad, the car of John~~, etc.

Possessive adjectives

1 We use possessive adjectives before a noun to say who something belongs to.

My name's Joanne.
Is this your pen?
He's my brother. I'm his sister.
She's nice. I like her smile!
The cat isn't in its bed.
We love our house.
Are the students in their classroom?

2 The possessive adjectives are:

Subject pronoun	I	you	he	she	it	we	they
Possessive adjective	my	your	his	her	its	our	their

this / that / these / those

1 We use *this* or *these* to point out things that are close to us. We use *that* or *those* to point out things that are not close to us, or are close to other people.

Look at this photograph – it's my sister.
These oranges aren't very nice.
That shop is a really good place for clothes.
We don't like those boys.

2 We use *this* or *that* with a singular noun. We use *these* or *those* with plural nouns.

this photograph   *that* house
these rooms   *those* tables

UNIT 4
there is / there are

1 *There is (There's)* and *There are* are used to say that something exists.

There's a small shop in our street.
There are two supermarkets near here.
There are lots of great shops in the town centre.

2 *There's* is the short form of *There is*. In speaking and informal writing, we usually say *There's*.

3 In positive sentences, we use *there's* with a singular noun and *there are* with plural nouns.

There's a cat in the garden.
There's an old lady in the café.
There are nice shops in this street.

4 In questions and negative sentences, we use *a/an* with a singular noun and *any* with plural nouns.

Is there a bank near here?   *There isn't a bank near here.*
Are there any restaurants here? *There aren't any restaurants here.*

some / any

1 We use *some* and *any* with plural nouns.

There are some good films on TV tonight.
There aren't any games on my tablet.

2 We use *some* in positive sentences. We use *any* in negative sentences and questions.

There are some nice trees in the park.
There aren't any places to play football here.
Are there any good shoe shops in the town?

Imperatives

1 We use the imperative to tell someone to do something, or not to do something.

Come here!
Don't open the door!

2 The positive imperative is the same as the base form of the verb.

Turn right.
Open the window, please.

3 The negative imperative is formed with *Don't* and the base form of the verb.

Don't listen to him – he's wrong!
Don't open the window – it's cold in here.

UNIT 5
Present simple

1 The present simple is used to talk about things that happen regularly or are usually true.

*I **go** to school at 8 o'clock every day.*
*She **watches** TV after school.*
*We **play** the piano.*
*They **love** chocolate.*

2 The present simple is usually the same as the base form, but we add *-s* with 3rd person singular (*he/she/it*).

*I **like** pizza.*   *He **likes** pizza.*
*They **live** in London.*   *She **lives** in London.*

3 If the verb ends with *o*, *sh*, *ch*, *ss*, *z* or *x*, we add *-es*.

go – he goes   finish – it finishes   catch – she catches
miss – it misses   fix – he fixes

4 If the verb ends with a consonant + *-y*, the *y* changes to *i* and we add *-es*.

carry – it carries   study – he studies   fly – it flies

5 If the verb ends with a vowel + *-y*, it is regular.

buy – she buys   say – he says

Adverbs of frequency

1 Adverbs of frequency tell us *how often* people do things. Adverbs of frequency include:

always	usually	often	sometimes	hardly ever	never

100%   0%

2 Adverbs of frequency come after the verb *be*, but before other verbs.

*I'm **always** hungry in the morning.*
*I **usually have** breakfast at 7.00.*
*He's **often** tired.*
*He **sometimes goes** to bed early.*
*They're **never** late.*
*They **hardly ever** go on holiday.*

Present simple (negative)

The present simple negative is formed with *don't (do not)* or *doesn't (does not)* + base form of the verb.

*I **don't play** tennis.*
*She **doesn't play** football.*
*My grandparents **don't live** with us.*
*My brother **doesn't live** with us.*

Present simple (questions)

Present simple questions are formed with *Do / Does* + subject + base form of the verb.

Do you like the film?   *Does Mike like shopping?*
Do I know you?   *Does she know the answer?*
Do your friends play   *Does your dog play with a ball?*
video games?

UNIT 6
have / has got (positive and negative)

1 The verb *have/has got* is used to talk about things that people own.

*I've **got** a bicycle. (= There is a bicycle and it is my bicycle.)*
*He's **got** a problem. (= There is a problem and it is his problem.)*

2 We use *have got* with *I/you/we/they*. We use *has got* with *he/she/it*. In speaking and informal writing, we often use the short forms: *'ve got / 's got*.

*My mother's **got** black hair and blue eyes.*
*My friends **have got** a nice cat.*
*We've **got** two fridges in our kitchen.*

3 The negative form is *hasn't / haven't got*.

*I **haven't got** a tablet.*
*This town **hasn't got** a park.*
*They **haven't got** a car.*

have / has got (questions)

We make questions with *Has/Have* + subject + *got*. Short answers use *has/have* or *hasn't/haven't*. Remember that we don't use contracted forms in positive short answers (e.g. NOT: *Yes, I've.*)

Have you got my book?   *Yes, I **have**.*
Has your father got brown hair?   *Yes, he **has**.*
Has the shop got any new DVDs?   *No, it **hasn't**.*

Countable and uncountable nouns

Nouns in English are countable or uncountable.

1 Countable nouns have a singular and a plural form. We can count them. We use *a/an* with the singular nouns. We can use *some* with the plural nouns.

*He's got **a house**.*   *He's got **two houses**.*
*There's **a picture** on my wall.*   *There are **six pictures** on my wall.*
*There's **an orange** in*   *There are **some oranges** in*
the fridge.   *the fridge.*

2 Uncountable nouns are always singular – they haven't got a plural form. We can't count them. We can use *some* with uncountable nouns.

*I like **music**.*   *Let's listen to **some music**.*
*I like Japanese **food**.*   *Let's eat **some** Japanese **food**.*

3 We don't use *a/an* or numbers with uncountable nouns.

NOT *a bread   an information   three works*

UNIT 7
can (ability)

1 We use *can/can't* to talk about ability.

*I **can** swim.*
*I **can't** drive a car.*
*He **can** play the guitar.*
*He **can't** sing.*

2 The form is *can/can't* + the base form of the verb. To make questions, we use *Can* + subject + the base form of the verb. (We don't use *do/does* with *can* in questions or negative forms.)

*It's very small – I **can't read** it. (NOT: I don't can read it.)*
***Can you play** this game? (NOT: Do you can play this game?)*

3 Short answers are *Yes, … can* or *No, … can't.*

*Can he swim? **Yes, he can.***
*Can you sing? **No, I can't.***

Prepositions of time

We use different prepositions to talk about time.

1 With times of the day, we use *at.*

*School starts **at** eight o'clock.*
*The train leaves **at** seven thirty.*

2 With months and seasons, we use *in.*

*It always rains **in** December.*
*We play football **in** winter.*

3 With days of the week, we use *on.*

*I go to the cinema **on** Saturday.*
*There's a test at school **on** Monday.*

UNIT 8
Present continuous

1 We use the present continuous to talk about things that are happening at the moment of speaking.

*Please be quiet – I**'m watching** a film.*
*They're in the dining room – they**'re having** dinner.*
*Dad's in his office but he **isn't working**.*
*Hey, Alex – **are** you **listening** to me?*

2 We form the present continuous with the present simple of *be* + the *-ing* form of the main verb. Questions and negatives are formed with the question/negative form of *be* + the *-ing* form of the main verb.

*I**'m watching** a film but I**'m not enjoying** it.*
*They**'re playing** football but they **aren't playing** well.*
***Are** you **having** a good time? Yes, we **are**.*
***Is** she **doing** her homework? No, she **isn't**.*

3 If the verb ends in -e, we omit the e before adding *-ing*. If the verb ends in a consonant + vowel + consonant, we double the consonant before adding *-ing*.

leave   *We're **leaving** now.*
get   *It's **getting** dark – let's go home.*

like / don't like + -ing

When we use the verbs *(don't) like, love, hate* and another verb, we usually use the *-ing* form of the other verb.

*We **love living** here.*
*I **like dancing** at parties.*
*She **doesn't like listening** to classical music.*
*They **hate going** to the theatre.*

UNIT 9

must / mustn't

We use *must/mustn't* to talk about rules.

1 We use *must* to say that it's necessary to do something.

*We **must leave** now.*
*You **must go** to the doctor.*

2 We use *mustn't* to say that it's necessary not to do something.

*You **mustn't tell** other people.*
*We **mustn't be** late.*

3 The form is *must/mustn't* + the base form of the verb. We don't use *do/does* in negative sentences.

*You must **ask** me first.*
*I mustn't **eat** a lot of food at the party.* (NOT ~~I don't must eat a lot of food at the party.~~)

can (asking for permission)

1 We often use *Can I* + verb to ask for permission (ask if it's OK) to do something.

*Can I **ask** a question, please?*
*Can I **watch** the match on TV now?*

2 We use *can* or *can't* to give or refuse permission.

*Can I **use** your phone?*   *Yes, you **can**.*
                              *No, sorry, you **can't**. I'm using it.*

I'd like … / Would you like …?

1 We use *would ('d)* + *like* to ask for something, or to offer something, in a nice way. It is more polite than *want*.

*I'd **like** a sandwich, please.*
*Would you **like** a dessert?*

2 *I'd like* is the short form of *I would like*. We almost always use it in speaking and informal writing.

UNIT 10

Past simple: *was / wasn't*; *were / weren't*; *there was / were*

1 We use the past simple form of *to be* to talk about actions and events in the past.

*It **was** a lovely day yesterday.*
*They **were** at school last Friday.*

2 We form the past simple of *be* like this:

Singular	Plural
I was	we **were**
you **were**	you **were**
he/she/it was	they **were**

3 We form the negative by adding *not* (*was not, were not*). In speaking and informal writing, we almost always use the short forms *wasn't* and *weren't*.

*I **wasn't** at home last night.*
*She **wasn't** at the party.*
*You **weren't** very happy yesterday.*
*They **weren't** with us at the concert.*

4 The past simple of *There is(n't) / There are(n't)* is *There was(n't) / There were(n't)*.

*There **was** a lot of rain yesterday.*
*There **weren't** any interesting programmes on TV last night.*

Past simple: *Was he …? / Were you …?*

We form questions by putting the verb before the subject.

Were you late on Monday morning?
Was she at the cinema with you?

Past simple: regular verbs

1 We use the past simple to talk about actions and events in the past.

*I **played** video games yesterday.*
*They **liked** the film on Friday.*

2 With regular verbs, we form the past simple by adding *-ed*. It is the same for all subjects.

*He **closed** the window.*
*The film **finished** after midnight.*
*You **phoned** me three times last night.*
*We **wanted** to see them.*

3 When the verb ends in *-e*, we only add *-d*. When the verb ends in consonant + *-y*, we change the *y* to *i* and then we add *-ed*.

*We **loved** the concert on Sunday.*
*They **studied** for a long time before the test.*

UNIT 11
Past simple: irregular verbs

1 Many English verbs are irregular. This means that the past simple forms are different – they don't have the usual *-ed* ending, for example:

go – went
make – made
give – gave
take – took
put – put

2 For every irregular verb, you need to remember the past simple form. There is a list of irregular verbs on page 128.

Past simple (negative)

We form negatives in the past simple with *didn't (did not)* and the base form of the verb. It's the same for both regular and irregular verbs. It's the same for all subjects.

talk   I **didn't talk**.
like   You **didn't like** it.
give   She **didn't give** me a present.
go   He **didn't go** to town.
take   We **didn't take** any photographs.
make   They **didn't make** any money.

Past simple (questions)

We form questions in the past simple with *Did* + subject + the base form of the verb. It's the same for all verbs (regular and irregular) and for all subjects.

see   **Did** I **see** you in town on Saturday?
do   **Did** you **do** the homework last night?
go   **Did** your brother **go** to the same school?
take   **Did** they **take** you to the theatre?

could / couldn't

To talk about ability in the past, we use *could/couldn't* + the base form of a verb.

*When I was small, I **could walk** on my hands.*
*We went to London but we **couldn't go** on the London Eye because it was closed.*

UNIT 12
Comparative adjectives

1 We use the comparative form of the adjective + *than* to compare two things.

*My sister is **younger than** me.*
*Australia is **smaller than** Brazil.*
*My new smartphone is **better than** the old one.*

2 With short adjectives, we normally add *-er*.

*new – new**er***
*quiet – quiet**er***

With adjectives that end in *-e*, we just add *-r*.

*nice – nic**er***
*fine – fin**er***

With adjectives of two syllables that end with consonant + *-y*, we change the *y* to *i* and add *-er*.

*easy – easi**er***
*healthy – healthi**er***

With adjectives that end in consonant + vowel + consonant, we double the final consonant and add *-er*.

*big – bi**gger***
*hot – ho**tter***

3 With longer adjectives (i.e. with two or more syllables), we don't change the adjective – we put *more* in front of it.

*expensive – **more expensive***
*dangerous – **more dangerous***

4 Some adjectives are irregular – this means they have a different comparative form.

*good – **better***
*bad – **worse***
*far – **further***

one / ones

1 Sometimes we don't want to repeat a noun. We can use *one* or *ones* in order not to repeat it.

*The pizza was delicious – I want another (~~pizza~~) **one**.*
*These shoes are very expensive – I want cheaper (~~shoes~~) **ones**.*

2 We use *one* to replace a singular noun, and *ones* to replace a plural noun.

*This red shirt is OK, but the blue **one** is nicer. (one replaces shirt)*
*I don't want to play these old games – let's buy some new **ones**.*
(ones replaces games)

IRREGULAR VERBS

Base form	Past simple
be	was
begin	began
buy	bought
can	could
catch	caught
choose	chose
come	came
do	did
draw	drew
drink	drank
drive	drove
eat	ate
fall	fell
feel	felt
find	found
fly	flew
get	got
give	gave
go	went
have	had
hear	heard
keep	kept
know	knew
learn	learnt/learned
leave	left

Base form	Past simple
light	lit
make	made
meet	met
pay	paid
put	put
read /riːd/	read /red/
ride	rode
run	ran
say	said
see	saw
send	sent
sing	sang
sit	sat
sleep	slept
speak	spoke
stand	stood
take	took
teach	taught
tell	told
think	thought
understand	understood
wake	woke
wear	wore
write	wrote